SENT
by an
ANGEL

A True Story of Tragic Loss
and Unexpected Love

KEVIN SKELTON

HAY
HOUSE

HAY HOUSE

Australia • Canada • Hong Kong • India
South Africa • United Kingdom • United States

First published and distributed in the United Kingdom by:
Hay House UK Ltd, 292B Kensal Rd, London W10 5BE. Tel.: (44) 20 8962 1230;
Fax: (44) 20 8962 1239. www.hayhouse.co.uk

Published and distributed in the United States of America by:
Hay House, Inc., PO Box 5100, Carlsbad, CA 92018-5100. Tel.: (1) 760 431 7695 or
(800) 654 5126; Fax: (1) 760 431 6948 or (800) 650 5115. www.hayhouse.com

Published and distributed in Australia by:
Hay House Australia Ltd, 18/36 Ralph St, Alexandria NSW 2015.
Tel.: (61) 2 9669 4299; Fax: (61) 2 9669 4144. www.hayhouse.com.au

Published and distributed in the Republic of South Africa by:
Hay House SA (Pty), Ltd, PO Box 990, Witkoppen 2068. Tel./Fax: (27) 11 467 8904.
www.hayhouse.co.za

Published and distributed in India by:
Hay House Publishers India, Muskaan Complex, Plot No.3, B-2, Vasant Kunj, New
Delhi – 110 070. Tel.: (91) 11 4176 1620; Fax: (91) 11 4176 1630. www.hayhouse.co.in

Distributed in Canada by:
Raincoast, 9050 Shaughnessy St, Vancouver, BC V6P 6E5. Tel.: (1) 604 323 7100;
Fax: (1) 604 323 2600

A catalogue record for this book is available from the British Library.

Previously published by Poolbeg Books Ltd, Dublin, 2010, ISBN 978-1-84223-440-2

ISBN 978-1-84850-300-7

Printed and bound in the UK by CPI Bookmarque, Croydon, CR0 4TD.

All of the papers used in this product are recyclable, and made from wood grown in
managed, sustainable forests and manufactured at mills certified to ISO 14001 and/or
EMAS.

DEDICATION

This book is dedicated to my first love, Mena, whom I love and miss to this day. No matter where I go, or what I do, Mena, I know that you will always be beside me, guiding me along the way.

CONTENTS

ACKNOWLEDGEMENTS

There are so many people I need to thank for their help and support over the years, and if I have omitted any names please forgive me. First, and most important, I have to thank my family; in particular my mum Maggie, who was there for me when I was at my lowest ebb. My mother never stopped in her quest to get me back on the right track, and I will always be grateful to her for that. And my father John (otherwise known as Jake): he's the quiet man who says very little, but with one look you can see what he is thinking. In all of my life, I can hold my hand up and say that I never saw my father being angry and I never heard him raise his voice in our home, but when he gave you that look, you knew to listen. Mum and Dad, you have always been there for me and it is very humbling for me to have parents like you, and I thank God you are still with me today.

I also want to mention Mena's mother and father, Paddy and Mary, who unfortunately have both since passed on, and all of Mena's family, who were a great support when I lost my wife. To my children Paula, Tracey, Ray and Shauna. I know you all went through a hard time losing your mother and I know that I also put you through hard times for many years after, but even if I don't tell you often enough, I can hold my hands up and say that I am very, very proud of each and every one of you and I love you with all of my heart. And I know that your mother would be very proud of you all if she were here today. You have all made good lives and careers for yourselves and I am the proudest father there is.

Maria was God-sent, along with Andreea, Nicoletta, Iulia and Gaby. The only person I can thank for these people coming into my life is not here with us today, and that is Mena. I would not be in the position I am now had it not been for her. The arrival of young Gabriella was a crowning moment for me, as I truly believe that she is an angel sent down from God, an absolute darling. I just hope that I live long enough to see her old enough to look after herself, and then God can do with me whatever he likes.

To Mena's brother, P J Logue, who stood as godfather to little Gaby, and to my brother Gerard and his wife, my sister-in-law Connie, who stood as her godmother. We are very grateful to both of you for your support.

To Romey and Veronica, who stayed with me on the day I lost Mena. Romey was a very special uncle to me, and what they both did for me through all of this heartache was unbelievable. Unfortunately Romey was also taken from us and life is not the same without him. There is yet another big hole now in all of our lives that simply can't be filled. I want to say a big thank you to Carl and Gwen Annies. Carl was my boss in the Nestlé factory and we became very good friends over the years. He is still my friend to this day. He was always there for me and I will never forget that.

There's not many a Catholic man in Northern Ireland who would say that a former British soldier was his best pal, but Carl, be assured that your friendship means the world to me.

I'd also like to thank the Gaelic Athletic Association (GAA) for the help and support they gave me after the atrocity. Myself and the GAA have often crossed swords on many issues, but I will never forget the help and support I got at that particular time from the county board, especially Paul Derris. Another good pal of mine was Willy John Dolan from Aghyaran. Willy was one of the many people who helped us financially at the time, and I am very grateful.

A huge thanks also goes to Dessie McGlinchey from Castlederg for his help over the years, and to Maeve Sheridan who organized a concert in Drumquin Social Centre and gave me the proceeds. It was very touching at the time and I was very humbled by it. She was always a lady and she will always be in my heart and my prayers. Thanks also to my sister-in-law Maggie, who helped Maeve that night, and to all the artists who played at the gig.

One man in particular who helped me in fundraising for Romania and was a personal friend, and a giant of a man in my eyes, was Patrick O'Kane of O'Ceathain Arms, otherwise known as 'Tom's'. Another man who helped with the Romanian cause was Eoin McKenna, who owned The Hunting Lodge in Baronscourt and who also ran a night of fundraising for Romania. I also want to thank Jimmy Buckley, who played in Drumquin Social Centre for half price to raise cash to bring the children to Northern Ireland; thanks also to Mick Flavin, John Farry, Seamus Lunney, Brendan Quinn, Ollie Harron and Marian Curry and to the late and the great Johnny Loughrey. Johnny was to play for me at a function one night and, despite getting sick and being unable to make it, he made sure the night still went ahead and sent a replacement. Then, when he got back on his feet, he offered his services yet again and, true to his word, he played a gig for us, despite his illness, and it is something I will never forget. He put his own bad health behind him and was there to help others, and he will always have a place in my heart.

Sean McMullen is another man whom I will never forget. Sean worked with me in Nestlé and, despite being very ill and eventually dying after a battle with cancer, that man made a long journey to visit me to pay his condolences. It was very touching and I will always be grateful to him for thinking of me when his own troubles were clearly far worse.

Special thanks to Dominic Kirwin, a well-known country-and-western singer in Northern Ireland, for his help when it came to fundraising; and thanks to the D'Arcy brothers who donated a lorry at the last minute just before Christmas 2009 to bring aid across to Romania. We were panicking right up until the end, as we had all the aid ready to go but no transport to get it where it was needed.

I also want to thank the St Vincent de Paul Society for their help in the weeks and months after the Omagh bomb; it was very much appreciated. And the RUC/PSNI and the British Army for their help at the time of the bombing itself. The way they treated us and my family's interests was second to none.

Sean O'Kane, the undertaker who looked after Mena, was very professional in carrying out his duties at the funeral, despite being so close a friend and carrying his own grief. And to Father Devine, who was parish priest at that time, your help and support during your time in Drumquin was fantastic. A word of thanks also goes to Dr Rodgers for his help at that time, and to Dr Paddy Scully, who was a friend before, after and still is to this day.

I also want to remember Mrs Slevin, God rest her soul, who helped me on the day of the bombing. Words cannot say how I felt for this woman, for when the devil came to Omagh, an angel was there to give a helping hand. She will always be remembered in my prayers for as long as I live.

Father Kevin Mullen was also an invaluable help on that day in August 1998. Up until this day, he is still helping us through our grief. I can't say enough about him. Not only is he a marvellous priest but he's also a marvellous person and I hope he gets the reward in heaven that he genuinely deserves. I feel very humble every time I see him, for I know it must have been hell for him on that particular day, and God bless him for being there to support us all.

Also, thanks to the ambulance and fire crews who had to deal with the most horrific scenes on the day of the bombing and whose support and aid were invaluable to those who suffered and those who lost.

Charlie and Kathleen McHugh, I will never forget your help on those nights when my drinking reached its peak, as you were always there with helping hands to make sure that somehow, whether it be yourselves or your daughter Caroline, you got me home safe and sound.

To Frank Mitchell who in September 1998 got me and Shauna into the Tyrone Minors' changing room in Croke Park after they won the All Ireland minor final. It was a day we will never forget. It meant so much to Shauna in particular. The Tyrone Minors were a great support to my little girl when she lost her mother, and that day meant the world to her and will live on in her memory forever.

To the people in RTÉ who gave Shauna and myself tickets for the corporate box for the All Ireland in 2003, where we proudly witnessed Tyrone beat Armagh in the final. As a sporting family, we were truly grateful for that gift. And to Don Mullen who got me tickets for the rest of the family and their friends on that particular day.

A word of thanks also goes to Brendan Collins, Henry Robinson, Charlie Kelly, Christopher McGale, J J Breen and to the staff at Omagh County Hospital, Altnagelvin Hospital in Derry and Dundonald Hospital in Belfast for all of their help with Shauna.

And to my old neighbours, Marion Radford, Mrs Devenney and Sarah McCanny, now deceased, who always looked out for me after Mena died, making sure that no matter how bad a state I was in, I didn't go a day without eating some food. It was people like these and my own mother who kept me going through those hard times when I thought I would never see a light at the end of the tunnel.

I also want to thank the Northwest Romanian Relief Fund, in particular Sean Boyle, Mickey Newton and Sean Young, for their help with bringing the children over from 1997 until 2003, and their help to this day in taking shipments out to Romania for me. I know they get a lot of abuse at times from people as they try to do their work, but I know their hearts are in the right place. Sometimes people don't take the time to stop and think about others, but these men are genuinely working to make things better in places where a mere £10 can work miracles. The work they have done in Fagaras is priceless and I wish them all the best with their future work abroad.

To Doina, the director of the orphanage in Fagaras; I hold you in the highest esteem, for when we went there your door was always open to us and it was a sad day when you left that job. You are a true angel and I thank you for everything you did for me when I was visiting Romania.

To the Northern Ireland Referees' Association, who sent me and the kids on a holiday to Tenerife in December 1998 as we tried to come to terms with losing Mena; and to the Fermanagh and Western Referees' Association, of which I was a member and who, along with the NI Referees Association, donated £4,000 towards the Romanian cause.

Thanks to my former employers, Nestlé, who paid for a headstone to be erected on Mena's grave when they knew money was short for us. Also to the workers' social club in Nestlé who raised £6,000 for the Romanian fund.

Thanks to the 'Drumquin Wolfe Tones' for making the tea and sandwiches on the day of the funeral in the local hall. Your support will not be forgotten.

I would also like to thank the media for keeping the atrocity in the headlines. I have no qualms in saying that the two governments would rather see it dead and buried, but thanks to the media this has never happened and hopefully with their ongoing help we will get some type of justice or somehow get to hear the truth about what really happened on that day.

And to Mark Durkan and Martin Reilly, two men who helped me with complicated legal issues, work permits and visas as I attempted to get on with my life in the years following the bombing. And to Tom from the Tara Centre who helped me get my life back on track.

I would also like to thank Ovideo Demitrean for his support in a very difficult time.

I have some very special people in my life now, apart from my own children, and they are my wee grandson Aran and my other grandchild Nicole. They are absolutely fantastic kids. When I have a bad moment, which we all do at times, all I have to do is think about you two, or go to visit you, and it really does makes my life worth living.

I also want to thank Yvonne Kinsella for helping me to get my story down on paper and for being my agent, and to Patricia Prizeman, her partner in the business.

Once again I have to acknowledge my wife Mena for initially bringing Andreea to Ireland in the first place, because if she hadn't I wouldn't have what I am lucky enough to have here today.

Last, but by no means least, I want to say a huge thank you to the thousands of people from all over the world who sent cards of sympathy and support and donations through the post to me after the bombing. I hardly knew any of these people and yet they felt it in their hearts to send their help on to us as a family. Until the day we die, we will always be truly grateful.

People say the world is a very evil place, full of wrongdoers, but I can honestly say that my attitude changed after that day in August 1998 when I saw how genuinely caring people were, from as far away as Canada and Australia, and it is terrible to think that it takes something horrific like a bomb and losing someone you love to appreciate how many good people, caring people, there are in the world. I have seen this down through the years in my efforts to raise funds to help the orphans in Romania, and it really helped me to renew my faith in mankind.

Let's all hope and pray that we live to see a truly peaceful world where everyone can live together in peace and harmony despite creed, colour or nationality.

As I found out myself, in the most unusual of ways, wherever there is life there is always hope.

REALITY
WRITTEN BY MENA'S DAUGHTERS

For twenty-five years in this broken land
Murderers thought of the bombs that they planned
And the quiet Westside where we thought we were safe;
Twenty-nine were taken along with our faith.
That Saturday morn, all was bright.
Shopping for clothes in the warm sunlight.
Everyone was there to share all the pain:
Drumquin, Omagh, Donegal and Spain.
No one cared when the news came in –
A bombscare in Omagh; what a sin.
To Market Street we went without fuss,
Not knowing what was awaiting us.
At three fifteen our future was said
And all of the world slowly bowed their heads.
Twenty-nine people died on that street;
Some lost arms, eyes, legs and feet.
Some were lucky, some survived,
Some were unlucky to watch someone die.
As screams for help, cries for the dead,
Many went home to lonely, empty beds.
To think back now I can see it all.
Who would have known how it all would fall?
A quiet place 'til someone breaks the law.
Protestants and Catholics both had to pay
For the foolish games by the IRA.
Now we live with my father, us sisters and brother;
For the fifteenth of August also claimed our mother.

Chapter 1

The Day My World Stood Still

I'll never forget the morning of Saturday, 15 August 1998 – unfortunately, for all the wrong reasons. I woke up to a beautiful sunny blue sky, probably the hottest day so far that year. It was glorious. But I felt awful. I had always suffered from back problems, but for some reason that week it seemed to be getting worse by the day, and on this particular day it had really begun to play up. I knew when I got up that morning that if I went into work I wouldn't last the day.

I had a job at the time in Moffatt's quarry, just up the road from our house in Drumquin. I'd worked there since being laid off from the Nestlé's factory a couple of years earlier. I was a lorry driver for Moffatt and it was a very handy job for me because it was so near home; but when you have a bad back and you have to deliver a few tonne of tarmac, it's a different story. When I rang in that morning to say I couldn't make it in, the boss asked me if I'd do just one job – taking a load up to Sion Mills, not too far away. I knew the job had to be done and there was no one else around to do it, so I forced myself to get up and I headed off.

As it turned out, the pain wasn't too bad and I got home just after midday, but I still wasn't feeling great. I was due to referee a match later that evening; it was the start of the soccer season, and the first match after the summer holidays, but the game for some reason was cancelled. I was glad that it wasn't going ahead, because I knew the only way to beat the pain was to lie down and relax; I knew it wouldn't go away quickly if I was running around a pitch.

Since I was going to be around for the rest of the day, my wife Mena asked me if I'd go into Omagh with herself and the girls to get some of the school uniforms. She didn't drive herself and although I was in a lot of pain I knew that she was eager to get the school stuff out of the way. Between football and work, it was very rare that I was around with the car and she obviously wanted to make the most of it. Omagh was just nine miles from Drumquin and we only ever went there two or three times a year. Like a lot of men, I'm not into shopping at all but we headed off anyway because I knew that once I took my time walking around there were a few things I could do in the town while the girls looked around. I wanted to go into the travel agents to see what the prices were like for flights to Romania. We had just had a young visitor from there, someone who had unexpectedly changed all of our lives overnight, and I wanted to see how much it would cost if Mena and I were to travel over to see what the place was like and to get to see this little child again – but more about that later.

I would go into the travel agents while Mena, Paula, who was 18 at the time, Tracey, who was 15, and Shauna, who was just 13, went looking for school stuff. Tracey was at secondary school in Dromore and Shauna was still at the local convent.

Paula, our eldest, had finished school and was waiting to hear if she'd got into college. She wanted to be a teacher. Ray, the second eldest of the four kids, was 16, but he wasn't with us that day as he'd gone off fishing with his pals. Like me, he wouldn't be one for walking around the shops for hours with a group of girls.

So, the plan for the day was to get school uniforms and school shoes for the two youngest ones so that Mena didn't have to worry about picking everything up at the last minute before they went back to school in September.

We arrived in town at around 1:55 p.m. I parked the car in the town, right outside the Royal Arms Hotel, and the girls went off to have a look around. When I finished what I had to do, I headed up to Russells clothes shop to see if they were there. There were only two shops in the town that sold the convent uniforms, Russells and Wattersons, but they weren't in either of them.

I knew that Mena had to get them their school shoes as well, so I headed off to look in Shoe Zone. As I walked in I spotted Mena, Tracey and Shauna there having a look around. They said that Paula had gone off shopping with her boyfriend. Mena wasn't too pushed on the brown shoes they had in stock because she said that they were only cheap and wouldn't have lasted them the full term. So we said we'd head off somewhere else.

As we made our way towards the front door of the shop, a traffic warden came in and said that there was a bomb scare at the courthouse, not too far from where we were, and asked if we'd all start making our way up the street, away from the courthouse. There was no big alert, no one panicking; it was all very calm. So we didn't really think much of it and we just walked out and up the road, casually chatting as we went along.

We didn't have bomb scares very often in Omagh. There used to be the odd one every few months, but compared to other parts of Northern Ireland we weren't plagued by them. It wouldn't have been that unusual to hear that a call had come in to the RUC, saying there was a device in some place or another. Nine times out of ten it would be a false alarm; so no one tended to panic.

I got into my car, which was parked just outside the shop, thinking that we were going to head on home, but Mena said we'd carry on, since we were in town anyway, and we'd get the school uniforms over and done with. None of us thought much about the possibility of a bomb at all. In fact, the only time we mentioned it was when we walked past a maroon-coloured Vauxhall Cavalier parked at the side of the road. For no reason at all, Tracey joked that the bomb could have been in that very car, and there we were walking past it, laughing and chatting.

I told the girls that I'd be back in a few minutes and then I moved our own car away up to the back of the hotel. When I arrived back, they were standing beside Wellworths and we went into Kelly's to buy wee knick-knacks like pencils, rulers and things for school. I was just about to pay for the stuff when a policeman came in and asked us if we would all mind moving farther down the street again, because they had started to clear the crowds a little farther down the road. So we headed up to the counter, paid for what we had in our hands and went on down to McElroy's shoe shop. There were no brown shoes there at all, so we crossed the street over into S D Kells. Little did we know that we were actually being moved straight into the mouth of the bomb.

By this stage I was getting fed up walking around with three women looking in shops. I said to Mena, 'I'm going to head into Mr Gee's next door.' Mr Gee's sold wee ornaments and knick-knacks. So off I went on my own.

I watched as Shauna went over to the counter with her mammy to ask for brown shoes. Then I went off into the next shop to have a walk around and kill a bit of time.

As I got halfway down, I stopped and thought that I'd better go back to the girls in case they did have what they were looking for and Mena didn't have enough money on her to get them. But as I turned to head for the door, the bomb went off.

I heard a massive bang – an ear-blowing, echoing sound. The front of the shop I was in had a full glass front and within a split second it was completely sucked out onto the street, shattering into what looked like a million pieces. I didn't have time to think; it was surreal. In a daze and somehow on automatic pilot, I just walked straight out onto the street, struggling to keep my footing over the mounds of shattered glass and into a cloud of thick smoke.

There was an eerie silence all around me, broken only by the sound of people sobbing in every direction. The town was just disintegrating in front of me. I could still see the impact of the bomb literally making its way down the street, its suction and vacuum gathering, and on either side of the road windows were shattering to pieces, in out, in out, in and out, until it reached the river, where the suction suddenly seemed to stop and everything just went dead. On my side of the road the windows were still splintering out and, as one went out on my side, the shop on the other side had its windows blown in, on top of anyone who happened to be in its path at the time.

There was smashed glass and broken bricks everywhere. I stood in shock and watched as the Cosy Corner, a pub at the bottom of the street, literally folded in like a book. In seconds I witnessed it collapse in on itself, ending up flat on the ground in a pile of ashes, glass and dust. Slevin's chemist at the bottom of the street caved in on itself, like something you'd see in an Arnold Schwarzenegger film. And it all seemed to be happening within seconds.

In a daze, I made my way through what was left of the big window in S D Kells and I immediately saw Mena lying in the rubble. I never noticed anything or anyone else, just Mena and her bushy brown hair. It was a very weird feeling, because it was as if it were all just happening to me and I was oblivious to everything and everyone else around me.

Mena was lying flat out on the ground, her white skirt with black polka dots covered in dust and debris. She was face down in the rubble and I could see that her legs were badly damaged. There were lumps out of both of them and they were all twisted. Yet there was no blood on her face at all, so she looked as though she was just unconscious. But as soon as I lifted her arm up from under the rubble to pull her towards me, it went limp. There was no power whatsoever left in it, and I knew there and then that she was dead. My stomach felt sick; it just somersaulted, as if I were going to be sick, but for some reason I didn't cry. I suppose I was just in shock.

I couldn't find Tracey anywhere around the shop and I knew that Paula was somewhere else on the street, but I honestly thought at that split second that young Shauna was buried underneath the rubble with her mum because she had been standing beside her when I walked away and Tracey had walked away from them to the back of the shop. I couldn't see Shauna, though – her clothes, her bright red hair – and in my heart I thought she was gone.

There was rubble and dust and glass everywhere and I started to push and shove things out of the way to try to find my girls. But what I thought was debris from the explosion were actually the limbs of other people who had been around my wife and girls when it all happened. What I initially thought were bits of furniture or shelving or lumps of carpet were in fact torsos, fingers, toes, arms and legs. It was the most sickening sight imaginable. It was as if I were having a nightmare; maybe I was going to wake up at any second and realize that none of it had happened at all. The scene around me was like a nightmare scenario, as if it weren't real, and yet I knew that it was.

Some of the people I touched were dead, some badly injured. I didn't have time to think, to look around, to help anyone else; I just wanted to find my daughters now, safe and well, and get them out of there as quickly as possible. I was still beside Mena but rummaging around, praying that the girls would still be beside their mammy. Looking back at it, I feel guilty that I wasn't able to help anyone else, but my mind was only on one thing and that was my family.

The first fireman on the scene was Paddy Quinn. I knew Paddy very well, as I'd refereed him for years in GAA (Gaelic Athletic Association) matches when he played full-back for Omagh and St Enda's. He came over to me, put his hand on my shoulder, and lifted Mena's arm. He held it for a minute, feeling for a pulse, even a faint beat, and then he just dropped it.

He said nothing. He simply put his hand on my shoulder again and walked away. And that confirmed what I already knew, that she was gone.

Police officers ran into the shop and took me down the street. I was totally numb, but every time they walked away from me I walked back down towards the shop again. My girls were missing and I had already lost my wife, so I wasn't letting the police, or anyone else for that matter, stop me from searching for my wee girls. I knew they were only concerned about the safety of everyone who had survived, and worried in case another explosion took place, but I had my own worries.

For two solid hours I ran up and down that street, praying that I'd find them, that I might hear one of them calling for me. My heart was racing and I felt sick. I felt like I could throw up at any minute. The smell of death was just indescribable. It will stick with me for the rest of my life. The only words I can think of to explain how bad the stench was, is stomach-turning. Bodies were burnt and smouldering all around us.

There was one man lying in the rubble beside us, and the bloke next to me said, 'That's not a man, it's a tailor's dummy from the clothes shop.' And I said to him, 'Well, if it is a dummy, I just saw it move.' I hope to God that man died, because I wouldn't have wanted him to survive like that. When I looked at his face, it just wasn't there. There were no features left and he was covered from head to toe in blood.

People were still frantically running up and down, dragging bodies from the rubble and trying to save as many people as possible. I knew that my wife was dead and there was nothing I could do to bring her back, but I had to find my children.

People were crying all around me, squealing, walking around sobbing, with blood flowing down their faces, arms, legs.

Policemen and -women and ambulance personnel were helping the wounded and carrying the dead out on hospital stretchers and makeshift stretchers. Everywhere I looked there was shattered glass, people sitting in shock and most in tears on the sides of the road. It was like a scene from hell against the backdrop of a beautiful blue sky.

There was black smoke everywhere and, as I was running around, debris was still flying in the air, being blown with the vacuum of the bomb, and what was left of the car that carried the bomb just missed me as it blew past over my head. I could very easily have been killed as well that day and my children left with no mother or father. As I walked along the street, the stench was woeful and a burst water mains was making the conditions even worse, as the water was flowing everywhere, resulting in people's limbs, shoes, handbags, blood, everything floating down the street. Despite the sectarian reason for murdering so many people that day, whether Protestant or Catholic, I remember thinking to myself that the blood running down that street was all the one colour; there was no difference. At the end of the day, we were all only human.

After two hours of constantly running up and down to the shop where my family last stood, I finally found Tracey, slumped down on her knees beside her mammy's body, holding on to her for dear life and sobbing. She had been down at the lower part of S D Kells on her own when the blast took place and she'd been knocked out with the force of the impact. When she came to, she panicked and made her way over to where she had last seen her mammy and sister, walking over dead bodies and dismembered limbs. She was very lucky not to have got any serious injuries, just cuts and bruises, but she was in a state of shock. I had to literally drag her away from her mother that day, and it was something I will never forget, dragging my 15-year-old daughter from her dead mother's body. But I couldn't let my emotions get in the way; it was as if I was working on auto-pilot and my main priority had to be saving the lives of my children – finding my other two girls and getting them safely out of the area.

No one knew if there was only one bomb or if a few had been planted around the town. The fear was that, at any given second, another one could have gone off and everyone who had believed they were lucky enough to survive could have been wiped out in an instant. I never thought of what could have happened next. I was just so grateful that I had one of my children back safely. But we still didn't know where Paula and Shauna were. Tracey was numb. We were both numb. She cried on and off and we both just stood there on the street in shock at what had happened and how in the blink of an eye our normal, average family had been destroyed.

At one stage as I ran down the street, I snatched a mobile phone from the hand of a man standing on the roadside whom I had never seen before. I rang my dad and told him that Mena was dead. Like me, he was in shock. But it was too late for anyone to do anything. All we could do was hope and pray that the girls were OK. He said that he would ring Mena's mother and the rest of the family for me. I handed the stranger back his phone, thanked him and just prayed that the other two girls would be OK. Years later I met that man again; his name, it turned out, was Gary Mullen, and we met again in the most unusual of circumstances, but on that day he was simply a stranger on a street whom I had never met before, but to whom I was very grateful. If he had not been standing beside me that day, I would have had no other way of contacting my parents to let them know what had happened.

As I stood there in a panic at the side of the road, a member of the GAA county board, Declan O'Neill, came over to me and did his best to try to calm me down. My brother Aidan had come down after the phone call to my dad, but he couldn't calm me either. I was absolutely hyper. It was a mixture of grief, shock, panic and tension, and no matter what anyone did for me, I was uncontrollable. I just wanted to be let loose to go and search for Shauna. I knew she was trapped somewhere in that shoe shop and I was sure that she must have been dead, trapped under her mammy. I still didn't know where Paula was, and even though I was worried sick over her as well I had a gut feeling that she was OK.

All of a sudden, as I fought to get through the crowds to go back down again, a priest, Father Kevin Mullen, whom I had never seen before, walked over to me and simply put his two hands on me, one on each shoulder. I swear to God, that man somehow welded me to the street; I was so rigid that I literally couldn't move. I don't to this day know how he did it, but somehow that priest managed to do what nobody else could do that day. He settled me down. As he laid his hands on me, I felt some sort of strange calmness come over me.

Mrs Slevin, who has died since, God rest her soul, came along and took me down to Charlie McAleer's pub along with Tracey. She got me a large glass of brandy and tried to keep me calm. I will never forget that woman's kindness and thoughtfulness that day. But I was sitting there in the pub with all sorts of stuff going through my mind and I couldn't rest easy. I needed to get back out and start searching again.

As I came out the door, this guy who was walking up along the far side of the street shouted over to me, 'Hey, Kevin; you have a wee ginger-haired girl?' I said, 'I have,' and he replied, 'Well, she's up in the hospital.' To this day I don't know who that man was. I had never seen him before and I never saw him again, but I can never express in words how I felt when he shouted over to me, in all of the turmoil that surrounded us, that my little girl was alive.

I headed straight up to the county hospital. My mother was already there; she'd come up from Drumquin, and she knew that Shauna was alive before I did. I didn't have a mobile phone with me so there was no way of anyone contacting me if news had come through. As I got to the hospital, they were getting Shauna ready to transfer her in a chopper to Altnagelvin Hospital in Derry.

I'd been told that she had suffered a lot of facial damage and needed to have a lot of surgery, so I just briefly spoke to her as they rushed her off for emergency surgery.

I didn't know how bad her injuries were at the time but I was just so grateful that she was alive and well. In my mind, once she was still alive, we could deal with whatever was to follow.

At that stage, Shauna had no idea that her mother was dead. The most important thing right then was to get her well. I didn't know where Paula was until I got to the hospital. It was only years later that she told me that she had been convinced that the whole lot of us were dead until she'd heard from someone on the street that Shauna was in hospital in Tyrone. She had known that her mammy was gone; someone else had broken that news, and she was heartbroken. But in her mind, just like myself for two whole hours, we were all dead, the same way I was convinced that Shauna was dead. Paula only found out that I was alive when she got to the hospital and saw me standing there. She had been at the far end of the town and luckily escaped without any serious injury. She hurt her back as she ran from the scene, but she was very lucky not to have been right in the eye of the explosion.

Paula and I only spoke recently about this, and I can only imagine what those children felt at that time. But in each of their little heads, all of their family was gone, wiped away in seconds. And throughout my search for Shauna and Tracey, all I could do was hope to God that Paula was OK, because she had gone off with her boyfriend to shop on their own and I had just prayed that they had been well away from where the explosion had taken place.

At that stage we didn't have time to stop and think about what had happened and why people weren't cleared completely off the streets if they had received two warnings. The police had only told people to head up to Market Street, but it had all been done so casually that no one batted an eyelid; no one thought for a minute that it was actually a serious warning. The police didn't seem very concerned and so no one thought anything of it.

People were too relaxed, too happy. It was the height of summer. Everyone was wearing T-shirts and shorts and the sun was beaming down. If there was such a thing as a day where you could imagine something bad was going to happen, this definitely wasn't one of them. It was glorious. And things could have been an awful lot worse, although on that day you couldn't imagine anything being worse. But there was a parade due in Omagh just a short time after the explosion and there were hundreds of kids and adults taking part, but someone was looking after them that day. Some higher force saved them, there's no doubt in my mind about that. They were held back for some unknown reason; if they had been there at the time of the bombing they would all have been slaughtered for sure.

It was a lottery that day as to who would die and who would survive. One man was actually standing in the doorway of Kells shop with his child when the bomb went off and neither of them got a scratch on them, even though they were right in the firing line. The way it was that day, one man could have walked clear of the impact and the man or woman right beside him might have been blown to pieces. No one knows why one man survived and the other man died.

One guy, Jim Sharkey, was in his shop across the street when the oil tank he had out the back just blew into the back of his premises, destroying everything that got in its way – and yet he was OK. The pub, the Cosy Corner, was totally destroyed and everyone believed that the barman, J J Maguire, was dead, but I knew he wasn't. Carrick School, which I had attended, were supposed to be having a reunion there that night and, thank God, J J had been setting up the bar for the big night. Not one person was killed in that pub, despite the damage done, and only God knows why.

It was hard for people who weren't there on the day who lost relatives and friends, but for the poor unfortunates who witnessed it, all I can say is that it was horrendous and it will stay with them for the rest of their lives. There was total mayhem.

Nobody knew what to do. There was nobody there who could possibly know what to do in a situation like that.

God help the emergency services; I hold them in the highest regard for the job they had to do that afternoon. I don't know how any of them got through it. And God bless Father Mullen for doing what he had to do. At the time of the bombing, Father Mullen was based in the Church of Christ the King in another parish, but not long after Mena died he ended up as parish priest in our own area of Drumquin. I built up a great relationship with him. He was a great man and he stayed with those families, praying and comforting them all night.

Once I knew the girls were OK, I had to concentrate on Mena. As soon as Shauna was shifted to Derry I was whisked off to the Omagh Leisure Centre, where all the other families were gathered, waiting for news about their loved ones. The children were brought back home. I knew there was to be no news for me. My wife was dead and that wouldn't change. But I wanted to see her, to be with her. I was told that all of the bodies recovered had been taken to Lisanelly Barracks, a British army base that was operating as an impromptu morgue.

There were hundreds of people gathered in the leisure centre, panicking, crying, worried sick about their relatives, wives, husbands, daughters, sons. People waited in the hope that things wouldn't be as bad as they seemed for them, thinking that the longer it went on, the more hope there was that they were OK – maybe taken to some hospital for treatment.

I suppose for many who were there that night, they thought that no news was good news. But my stomach was sick. I knew my life was ruined and I could do nothing about it. There was no way back. There was a fella there called Kevin McCann, who used to work with me in the Nestlé factory, and he came over to me and asked me why I wasn't going up to look at the list and I told him I had no need to go; I knew that Mena was dead. Unfortunately, all I had to do was wait until whatever time they needed me to go in and identify her. As people gathered whenever a new list of names was put up on the wall, telling people who had been taken to which hospital, I just sat there. I had no reason to look because I had no reason to hope.

Maybe it made it easier for me at the time because most of those people in that room that day were hanging on in the hope of hearing that their loved one was alive, had survived, whereas I knew mine hadn't. The sad part of it all was that I knew most of the people there. I knew Godfrey Wilson and his wife, I'd worked with them in Nestlé's; their daughter Lorraine was killed. I knew Brian McCrory and his family; I'd worked with Brian, too, and he was standing right beside the car where the bomb exploded. He had been in town shopping for paint.

The killings crossed all sectarian divides: seven of the dead were mothers, six teenagers, two babies, three young boys from the same Donegal village, a 12-year-old exchange student from Madrid and his teacher, a Unionist official and his son, a Mormon schoolboy, a young woman pregnant with twins. I knew the majority of those people who were killed, or their families, except of course for the Spanish people and the children from Buncrana who were up for a day's shopping. It was a living nightmare. Over 300 people were injured, a young girl was blinded and many, many others lost limbs.

I stayed in that leisure centre all night with my uncle Jerome, God rest him, Romey as we called him, and his wife Veronica. And at ten o'clock on the Sunday morning I was eventually called out and taken to the barracks to see my wife. We were brought into a tent, one of many makeshift mortuaries set up to house the bodies of those killed, and they brought Mena's remains in on a stretcher.

I remember walking in on the left-hand side of her body and Veronica and Romey walking up along the right-hand side. As they pulled the sheet down, Veronica collapsed on the spot. I just looked down at my wife lying dead, cold and stiff, and confirmed that yes, it was my wife, and that was it. They covered her up again and we went home, devastated.

It was the most unusual feeling because I had known all along that Mena was dead, but to see your wife laid out on a stretcher, grey and cold, covered up with a sheet, is a different story altogether. You realize there and then that there is no going back. You know that your life with the woman you love is gone forever. You'll never see her, talk to her, walk with her, hold her hand, ever again. And what made it worse for me was that she looked perfect, no marks; she was lying there just as if she were asleep. She was only 39 years old and still had her whole life ahead of her, but in an instant that was all taken away.

It killed me to have to leave her there, alone again, but I had no choice. I had to try to be strong for the rest of the family. I just didn't realize how hard that was going to be. When we headed out of the leisure centre that day, I drove up to the hospital to see Shauna. I met a good friend of mine there. His daughter had lost half of her leg and I hadn't known. I hadn't heard a thing about her. I stood talking to him for a few minutes, and of course he was devastated like us all. He said he was sorry to hear about Mena, and then I went on in to see Shauna.

That day I had to do the hardest thing I have ever had to do: I had to tell my little girl that I had some bad news for her and that her mammy was dead.

My stomach was sick just thinking about how I was going to break it to her and how she would take it. I knew she had enough to deal with right then with her own injuries, but I couldn't put it off. I knew that if I didn't say it, someone else would let it slip and then it would have been ten times worse. I just didn't want to have to break it to her as she lay on a hospital bed surrounded by strangers.

When I finally got the words out, she looked up at me with tears in her eyes and said, 'I know, Daddy. I knew before I left Omagh Hospital. I asked my nana, "What about my mammy?" She said, "I think your mammy might be OK," but I knew by Nana's face that Mammy was dead.'

I didn't know what to say to her. It was tough, it was very tough for me. Shauna was just 13 years old and her mammy probably saved her life that day, because she would have taken most of the blast as she stood in front of her. And Shauna knew that as well, so it was even harder for her to accept that her mother was gone and she would never see her again. I stayed for a while with her that day but I knew that I'd have to go back to the house to the others at some stage. I didn't want them left on their own, either. I was totally caught between a rock and a hard stone, as they say.

Shauna seemed to be coping well, despite some horrific facial injuries all down one side of her face. She spent seven hours in one operation in Altnagelvin Hospital as surgeons tried to get the splinters and shards of glass out of her little face. She spent a week there in total and then she was transferred to the hospital in Dundonald, where she had more operations to remove the glass from her neck.

She had to undergo a number of procedures after that as they tried to save as much of her face as they possibly could, but she was being so brave, so strong. Every time I came in, her face was covered up with gauze and she never once let me see the damage. She was a very courageous little girl for her age. I think she knew that I was devastated at the fact that Mena, her mammy, was gone, and she didn't want to upset me any more. I'm convinced of that. She didn't mind me leaving her in the hospital because she knew that I had to be at the house to meet people.

She was the youngest in the ward; most of the girls were 17 or 18 and older and had their mammies with them, but she never let the fact that her mammy was gone get to her. Or if she did, she never let me see it.

Back home, the crowds had started coming to the house from very early on the Sunday – as soon as the news broke that Mena had been killed. They came from all over the place to offer their condolences. My mother Maggie was staying in the house to help us out and to look after the kids, and she was there all the time to welcome people and accept Mass cards and words of sympathy on behalf of us all. People understood that I had other things to do and they just wanted us to know that they were thinking of us, even if I wasn't able to be there in person to thank them.

On the Sunday morning, when the family woke up and pulled the blinds, we found a TV crew had a camera set up in the back garden and they had never even asked permission from any of us to film, let alone come onto our property. One of the lads went out and told them in no uncertain manner to get out of there. There were a lot of reporters who came ploughing up to the door and they wanted an interview, no matter what. They had no sympathy, no respect for how we were all feeling. It took a lot of patience for me not to hit them, to be honest, because I could not believe that anyone could be so ignorant and uncaring. But I held my cool and did what I had to do.

The days leading up to the Tuesday, when I was due to bring Mena home, dragged on. We all felt as if the day would never come because all we wanted was to have her back home with us, no matter how hard it would be for us to have to deal with it. As I sat in the car in the driveway on the Tuesday, I had this strange thought that maybe, for some reason, when we got to take Mena home, we wouldn't be able to see her. So I went back into the kitchen and said to my mother, 'Don't be one bit surprised if when we get Mena home we won't be able to open the coffin.' I don't know why I thought that, because when I had seen her she looked fine; but I just had this odd feeling. No one had mentioned the possibility of it happening before.

Indeed, when we got there, the undertaker, Sean O'Kane, whom I had known for years, said, 'Kevin, you can't open the coffin; she is too badly damaged.'

I thanked him for all he had done. I understood how hard it must have been for him working there, looking at all these people lying dead in front of him whom he knew so well. It broke my heart that I couldn't see my wife for the last time and that our children couldn't say a proper goodbye to their mammy, but there was nothing I could do.

We brought her home and the grief was indescribable. We were all in bits.

On that day I stood outside my house from 2:00 p.m. until 2:00 a.m. the following morning, shaking hands with people. They actually queued up the street for hours on end, and when they got to the house they went in and up the stairs to where I had Mena laid out in our bedroom in a closed coffin on our double bed, with our wedding photo and a trophy that I had won when I was playing darts in 1978 on the coffin lid. They had run a competition for me in Drumquin, to give me money for a wedding present, and I ended up winning the trophy that night, so I buried it with Mena. It was something that was special to me and I wanted her to have it with her.

The visitors just never stopped coming that day. There were also some people who arrived on my doorstep, and if I'd had a shotgun I'd have gone for them, hook, line and sinker. But fair play to my mother, she calmed me down and told me to leave it alone, that it wasn't worth it. And so I let them go in and I let them see for themselves the damage that was done. I knew they were there for one reason and one reason only – to dissociate themselves from what had happened in Omagh. But for Mena's sake and for the sake of the kids, I kept my mouth shut. I realized that it wasn't the time or the place to air my feelings. I knew that I had to respect my wife and I reluctantly agreed to shut my mouth and save my feelings for another time.

I was stunned by the number of people who arrived to pay their last respects. Mena would have been mortified. She was a very quiet lady, a lovely woman, and everyone who knew her liked her. I was delighted for her that so many people came to show they cared.

On the day of Mena's funeral I was left in shock at the number of people who turned up at the church in Drumquin. I had
thought that with so many coming to the house, there would
be less of a crowd at the church, as people had work to go to
and families to take care of. But Mena was the only person
who was still living in Drumquin at that time who was killed.
Another family, the McFarlands, lost their little girl Samantha;
her mother was originally from Drumquin but had moved out
years before, but we all knew the family well, as it was a very
tight-knit community.

There were other funerals taking place on the same day all
around the county, but there must have been about 7,000 people
at the church for Mena's mass. There were busloads from Cavan,
because one of her sisters was married and living in Cavan; there
were referees from Dublin, Kerry, Cork, all over Ireland. I never
saw anything like it in my life. In fairness to the TV crews that
day, I told them they could follow us for about two kilometres to
the church, but when the coffin was taken into the church they
were to leave. They did what I asked that day.

After the burial in the old graveyard at St Patrick's Church
in Langfield, everyone started to queue up to shake my hand,
but there were so many people there that morning that by the
time we were finished, I had to put my right hand into my
pocket and shake hands with my left, because my arm and hand
were aching so much. It was unbelievable. There will never be
anything like it in Drumquin again.

I often wondered around that time why it wasn't me and
not Mena taken that day. But I know that if it had been me,
Mena could never have coped with the crowds. I thought to
myself as I stood there looking around the graveyard that if

Mena had looked up from her coffin and seen the number of people around who were coming up to shake my hand, she'd have gone down a mouse hole. She would have been mortified; she was just too quiet for all that attention.

Once again, on the day of the burial, some politicians arrived that I didn't want there, but once again I accepted them for that day. We had more than 2,500 Mass cards and letters sent to us from all over the world, from as far away as Australia and Canada. I was very touched by it; we all were. But I got one bad letter, about three or four days after the funeral, from somebody in Ireland who claimed he knew who had carried out the bombing. I found out later that a lot of families had received the same letter. It turned out that he was just some head-case. At first I didn't know what to think, that maybe it was genuine and that we'd have a breakthrough quickly, but another family passed their letter on to the police and they, in turn, came to me and we realized quickly that it was just a madman. It was hard to cope with that, but you just had to move on.

On the other hand, there were so many people out there who supported us after it happened. We got cash donations from everywhere and it helped us so much to get over that first year. I'm sure most people won't have had any idea how it helped, but it got us by that year. I couldn't bring myself to go back to work and we were really struggling, so if it wasn't for the thoughts and generosity of many people, whom I didn't even know, I would not have got through those first 12 months or so. The GAA and the Football Association of Ireland were fantastic as well. Even players whom I would have taken abuse from over the years as I refereed games came to me and offered their condolences.

I was offered a trip to Lourdes at the time and I would have loved to go, but there was another memorial service coming up at the same time and so I couldn't make it to Lourdes. Of all the offers we received, I wished so much that I could have gone on that particular trip, as I had heard so much about how peaceful a place it is. It would have been nice to go and say a prayer for Mena.

Around the same time I also received a letter from a woman in Canada, Olive McMenamin, whom I had gone to school with many years before and hadn't seen in decades. She invited me and my family out for a holiday to get away from things. We didn't get there either, unfortunately, but the offer was very surprising and very much appreciated.

Shauna was in hospital for about two weeks after the bombing. She was allowed out for her mammy's funeral, just for a couple of hours, and she went back that evening. The kids were absolutely distraught that day, as we all were. We just couldn't believe it had happened to us. But we all stood tall together and tried to be as dignified as possible for Mena. It was extremely difficult, but all of our families and friends supported us and were there for us day and night.

We knew that we would never see Mena again, and although we were devastated, we had no choice but to turn our attention to taking care of Shauna and making sure that she was OK. When I'd visit her in the ward, she'd say to me at 2:00 p.m., 'Now, daddy, you go home now.' She'd give me a list of things to do – what to put in the washing machine, what to buy in the shops. She was a fiery little redhead and she was taking over the role of 'mammy'. Even though she was the baby, she took control immediately and tried to keep me in place. She'd give me two hours after I'd leave the hospital and then she'd ring me on my mobile and ask where I was. And if I wasn't at home, she'd order me home. She has kept me on my toes ever since. In the days and weeks that followed, I found it very hard to cope and I ended up spending my days propping up the bar in a pub instead of being at home with my family. Shauna was making sure that I didn't get away with it lightly.

It had been very hard for her on the day of the funeral to go back to a ward and leave her family behind. She was lucky to have been allowed out for the day at all, but I know that she would never have coped if she had missed her mother's funeral.

After the burial, when the crowds of mourners left the house and we were left as a family on our own, there was an inexplicable silence, as if we shouldn't talk about it. We all just sat around saying nothing. Maybe we all felt that if we didn't discuss it, then we wouldn't have to accept it immediately, because we were still trying to come to terms with what had happened. At that time it still felt as if it wasn't real and that at any moment we would all wake up and realize that it was just a very bad dream and Mena would still be there. She'd walk into the room and laugh at how upset we all were, make us believe that it was all a bad joke; that nothing had happened after all.

The three older children automatically stepped into the breach in the days that followed and took control of everything. They worked together and kept the house going for us all, with the help of my mother and my family.

When I think back on the day of the bomb, I remember how it had been one of the most beautiful days of the year, and how everyone around, just minutes earlier, had been in good form. People were walking around with smiles on their faces.

The sun was shining and everything was perfect, until ten minutes past three on that Saturday afternoon.

When the explosion took place it felt like time just stood still. Everything had suddenly come to a standstill. And in a split second and without a thought from those responsible, the lives of so many people were destroyed, forever.

PRECIOUS TEARS
BY GERRY SKELTON

In many silent little graveyards
Amidst the green fields of Tyrone
Sleep the loved ones, now the victims
That leave shattered broken homes.
Sent to a brutal death in Omagh
By a voice from Hell on the telephone.
Mothers and daughters, fathers and sons,
Brothers and sisters, babies so young,
Workers who tended the shops all around,
Friends happy, laughing, just a day in town.
Now a heartbroken man with two children will mourn
A wife and mother with twin babies unborn.
For everyone that day had started so bright;
Fun and laughter in warm sunlight.
Sure there was peace, nothing to fear;
Choosing clothes and shoes for the new school year.
The traders of Omagh welcomed them all –
Young children from Spain, their friends from Donegal.
The lying phone call was precise, loud and clear.
All worked hard to get the street clear.
Near the courthouse, at the top of the town
The timer of a bomb was fast counting down.
But the bomb exploded far away from this hill;
In crowded Market Street twenty-nine did it kill.
The dark cloud of smoke now over the town
Would not mask the carnage on the blood-coloured ground.
Screaming, demented, many out of their mind,

Searching the rubble, loved ones to find.
Where is the peace in this tortured land
For the child who is clutching her dying mum's hand?
Those seven and twenty caskets carried shoulder high
Past stunned, bewildered relatives who softly say goodbye.
Then two tiny white coffins of babies so dear;
Even God in his Heaven must have then shed a tear.
Shall innocent mites have died just because
Evil hearts still chase a God-forsaken cause?
In the churches and chapels the prayers have been said
To ask strength for the living, peace for the dead.
The reporters are gone, their talents well used
Treated all with compassion, no trust did they abuse.
And a fond mother's love, young children did lose;
A terrible price for a new pair of shoes.
In a little house indoors, beside the chapel hill,
A favourite chair stands empty, the knitting needles still.
Now many sad children face long empty days
That a mother once filled with her loving ways.
Now on lonely dark nights, they will softly weep
For that precious love, they could not keep.

21 August 1998

Chapter 2

Meeting Mena

When I was in my prime, young, free and single, I used to play a card game called twenty-fives every Wednesday night in the wintertime at the home of a friend of mine called Paddy Mimnagh. Eight of us would get together each week, and the craic we'd have was unbelievable. It was the 1970s.

At the time, Paddy was going out with a girl I didn't know, Theresa Logue. On one particular night he arrived with Theresa, whom he actually ended up marrying, and this lovely girl with long curly hair. I had never seen her before and I remember staring at her all that night, because she was absolutely beautiful. I remember thinking at the time how naturally gorgeous she was – no fancy clothes or face covered in make-up. She was just a natural beauty. I sat there all night and never spoke to her once. I just didn't have the confidence to say anything, and sure I wouldn't have known what to say to her anyway, because it was the first time I had met her. Her name was Mena, short for Philomena.

I thought about her non-stop after that night. Then, two nights later, on the Friday, I went down to the local dance in the

Drumquin Social Centre and, lo and behold, there she was. I even remember who was playing that night: it was Big Tom and the Mainliners, a band that was very popular back then. Any venue they played at that time would be packed to the rafters. Everyone went to the local dances in the little towns because Omagh during the Troubles was blocked off with barriers at night-time, as they tried to keep the troublemakers out and avoid any problems. If you wanted a drink and a dance after hours, then you had to go outside of Omagh itself. So people came up to our area and went to the pubs before the dance, because there was no alcohol allowed in the hall, and then after the dance you went back down to the town again before you went home. It seemed like Drumquin never closed in those days. It was nine miles from Omagh and anyone who came to the dance was guaranteed a good night. The women used to line up on one side of the hall and the men on the other, and there would have been 1,300 or 1,400 people there that particular night.

Yet I spotted her immediately.

I thought to myself that, one way or another, I was going to approach her that evening for a dance, because if I didn't, someone else would do it and it would be too late. However, I walked across that floor six times that night to ask her to dance, and each and every time, when I got to within a few feet of her, I'd turn back. I was so angry with myself for being so stupid. I just couldn't believe that I didn't have the courage to talk to her.

Once again she was on my mind all that week. I was kicking myself for not just asking her up onto the floor. But the following Friday I went up to the hall again, hoping she might be there. I thought it odd that, in all the times I had been to that dance over the years, I hadn't spotted her before, but I had made my mind up that no matter what happened this particular night, if she was there, I was asking her up.

And yet I did exactly the same thing again. I walked towards her time and time again, but I just couldn't bring myself to open my mouth. I ended up going home again that night feeling like a right fool and regretting not having the guts to go over and say hello. It wasn't like me at all, because normally if I liked a girl I wouldn't think twice about asking her for a dance. Somehow, this girl was different.

The following week, on the third Friday night, I went down with a pal of mine, Dessie Fanthorpe, to Pat Roe's bar in Drumquin for a soft drink or two before we headed off to the dance. At that time I didn't drink alcohol, but Dessie sneakily slipped a bit of vodka into my Coke without me even realizing it. Sure, by the time we got to the dance, I was in great form. I had so much confidence with the booze in me that I could have taken on the world. And when we walked in the door, there she was, standing there looking gorgeous as always. So, with the alcohol in me, giving me a bit of Dutch courage, I marched across the floor, not a bother on me, and asked her up to dance. And she accepted.

That was October of 1973. She was just 14 years old and I was 19. She was very young, some would say too young for a man of 19, but she looked older than she was and I genuinely thought at the time that she was about 16 or 17. When she eventually told me how old she really was, I was shocked. She didn't act like a 14-year-old at all and neither of us felt awkward about the age difference, so we just chose to ignore it and carried on going out together. We got on great and that was all that mattered.

I used to go and pick her up after school at St Mary's in Irvinestown and we'd head off for a while on our own. I was working as a labourer with McGinn and Sons at the time, who were building houses in the area. I had a nice few bob coming in and I drove a Hillman Hunter 1725, with one of those big long aerials on the roof. You were supposed to clip the aerial down when you drove to stop it hitting anything, but I never bothered. I would be driving that car so hard that the aerial would have been smashing off everything it came in contact with on the road at full speed and it was destroyed; but it still managed to get all the radio stations in.

Mena loved our little drives into the countryside because it meant we were away from everything and everyone. We'd just go for little jaunts and listen to the radio. I'd fill her in on what I had been up to that day and she'd yap on about what had happened in school. It was all innocent fun. Then I'd meet her every Friday night at the dance. We didn't really get to go out on dates much at the time because she was so young and couldn't tell her parents what she was up to, so we had to make the most of whatever little opportunities arose, like our short drives after school before she got stuck into her homework.

Her parents didn't know about us for a long time. Every Sunday night, her father Paddy and her mother Mary used to go to the bingo up in the hall in Drumquin. I knew exactly what time they left every night. Her mother drove an old Mini and she never put that Mini into third gear. She was an awful driver to get stuck behind, so I knew that she'd have to leave at a certain time if they were to make it to the bingo on time.

As soon as they'd go out that door, I'd be up there to see Mena and we'd sit together, maybe watch a bit of telly and relax, chatting about everything and nothing. I'd know how long it would take her parents to get home, so I'd be well away before they got back again. Mena's younger sister and two brothers would have been in the house but they never ratted us out to their parents. Mena had them well warned.

I knew that I had strong feelings for this young girl right from the start. We just seemed to get on really well. It turned out that Mena was the younger sister of Paddy Mimnagh's girlfriend Theresa and that's how she had come to the house that night when we were playing cards.

It was great having Theresa going out with Paddy, because it meant that Mena and I could go out with them as another couple when they were going to the dances. Theresa and Mena got on very well. When herself and Paddy went to a dance in Pettigo, Mena would go along with them. Her parents never thought anything wrong in it because they saw her go out with Theresa and come back with Theresa later in the night. This little plan was grand and a handy way for us to meet up with no suspicions raised.

It took some time before I finally got to meet the family, but when I eventually got my feet under the table I got on very well with her Da. In time, he became like a second father to me. They lived in a place called Kesh, which was classed as a very Loyalist area. Even the footpaths were painted in red, white and blue or with the Union Jack. I'd often take her father off to a bar in Pettigo, just a few miles from where their house was, to have a few shots of black rum. Mena's mother wasn't happy with me taking her father out, but I didn't care, because I loved going out with him. He was an absolute gentleman and he called a spade a spade. He was a very calm man and everyone who knew him spoke well of him. None of the other girls' boyfriends ever took Paddy off for a drink, and they were all afraid of Mary, but she didn't worry me.

There were nine children in Mena's family, but one of the girls, Ann, died when she was only a baby, leaving eight of them living. They were all very close. Paddy loved going out for a few jars and it gave him a break away from the house and the kids. He was a very genuine person and I'll never forget him. He died before Mena was killed and I was glad that he wasn't around at the time, because I know he would have found it very difficult to cope with. Her mother was heartbroken.

They had already lost another daughter, Kitty, the eldest child, who had died of cancer when she was a young woman. It's very difficult for any parent to lose one child, never mind three in total, two when they were grown women. Kitty was married to a man called Charlie McHugh, one of the very first heart transplant patients in Papworth Hospital in London. Unfortunately, he lasted no time after the surgery and then, when everyone thought things couldn't get any worse, Kitty got cancer and died. It was a horrible time for the family.

Mena was a very loving, quiet person. While we got on great, to be perfectly honest, we were like chalk and cheese.

They say opposites attract and there was no doubting that we were total opposites. What I was interested in, she wasn't. With me, it was darts and football, and she wasn't into either of them. She wasn't even keen on going around to the pubs when I'd be playing in a darts match. But I remember one night when I did convince her to come off with me. It's a night I'll never forget.

We were playing in The Crescent Inn in Castlederg and I persuaded her to get dressed up and come along, even though she knew hardly anyone who'd be there. She sat nearby on a leather seat, beside another woman whose husband was playing darts. Then this girl came in, the daughter of the other woman, and sat down between her mother and Mena. The young girl staggered into the seat and everyone knew that she was the worse for wear. She was falling around the place and her mother was trying to keep her still. But she was so drunk that she actually wet herself. She peed all over the chair and the urine ran right down along the leather seat and right in under Mena.

Mena's face was priceless that night. She stood up, because she could feel something wet underneath her, and suddenly she realized that she was absolutely soaking wet; her skirt was drenched and you could smell the urine off her. All she wanted to do was to go home. She was nearly in tears and she never went back to that pub after that. In fact, she hardly ever went to darts matches anywhere after that night. I thought it was hilarious but Mena was mortified and worried sick that other people there would have thought that it was her who had wet herself, as she was the one walking around with a wet skirt and the one who ended up going home early. She thought the darts crowd were too rough anyway and, to be honest, some of them were. But I always enjoyed these nights out. It just wasn't Mena's cup of tea.

We were going out together for about five years before we became man and wife. I had planned all along to ask her to marry me. I actually proposed to her as we sat in the car one night and she immediately said 'Yes'. I wasn't the sort of fella for roses and going down on one knee back then and she knew that. There was nothing at all romantic about me in my twenties, but we made it all happen in County Donegal.

My brother Aidan was playing for Tyrone Vocational Schools in the Gaelic Athletic Association (GAA) and we all went up to Dublin for the All-Ireland final, where Dublin were playing Kerry. We slept all night in the car on the Saturday because we couldn't get a place to stay, as there was some other big game on that weekend as well and every guesthouse was full. We went to the game on the Sunday and when it was over Mena and myself headed to Mullingar, where we stayed overnight in a bed and breakfast. We were so wrecked when we arrived that we slept like babies from the time we put our heads on the pillows. We had planned to go off for a few days' break on our own, so the next day we headed off to Salthill in Galway, where we stayed for another couple of days. We were having a great time and we finished off the break with a night in Bundoran in County Donegal.

I knew Mena was enjoying herself. In Bundoran we talked about what she would like for our big day and whom we would invite, and she was getting all excited about it. So we went into the town to look at some rings and she chose her own in a shop called Gilhooleys in the town centre. I had been pestering her for ages about getting married and having kids and we both knew that we were going to be together for the rest of our lives, so getting engaged was a natural thing for us both.

We were delighted with ourselves to be getting hitched and Mena couldn't wait to get home to tell her family and show off her engagement ring. She was so excited, but she was also very nervous about how they would all react back home to the news. She was still very young – just 17 – and I had to accept that I was a good bit older than her, but we were in love and that was that.

Just as I had expected, her father was delighted when he heard the news, and so were her brothers and sisters, but I know for a fact that her mother wasn't happy at all. She never actually came out and said it to me but it was written all over her face. Maybe she thought that Mena was still too young, I'm not sure, but she knew that we were in love and that Mena was happy, and so she didn't really argue with us.

Mena was dying to get started, organizing everything. She was looking at dresses and talking about the invite list and what we'd have to eat and what band we would have and how much it was all going to cost. Her sisters were all advising her and everyone got involved. We set a date for 31 August 1978 and we married in St Joseph's church in Ederney, County Fermanagh, the day before Mena turned 20. It took a whole two years to plan, but it was worth every minute of it. We invited about 80 people and we held the reception in The Silver Birch Hotel in Omagh.

Mena looked absolutely beautiful that day. I remember watching her coming down the aisle and I was the happiest man in Ireland. I knew that we would be happy for the rest of our lives and we were both madly in love.

Her sister Caroline was our bridesmaid and Gerard, my brother, was our best man. It was a fantastic day, one of the best days of my life. We planned our escape that night from the reception by leaving our car in a place known only to Gerard. We knew that if the car had been left openly on display it would have ended up with tin cans streaming out of the back of it and lipstick marks all over the windscreen telling everyone we were 'Just Married', so we only told the one person that day.

We picked up the car at the end of the night and headed to

Monaghan town, where we stayed overnight in the plush Four Seasons Hotel, just on the outskirts of the town. We were on a high and looking forward to the start of our lives as a married couple. I remember how we had a room full of wedding presents that we could have made a fortune from if we'd had an auction. We got the usual back then – electric kettles, irons, sets of knives, dinner services, blankets and sheets and four radio alarm clocks, which were the 'in thing' at the time; if you got one you were delighted, but we got four.

When I look back at how weddings have changed over the years, I have to laugh, because nowadays you have to give a present worth at least €150 or you'd be talked about. There's no such thing as handing over a cheap kettle or an iron any more, unless it's state of the art and it also makes your breakfast and hangs the clothes on the line. Yet we were so grateful back then for anything we were given; that's how hard times were.

We spent our honeymoon in Scotland. We had planned to tour the country, because I had heard so much about the place and was dying to see what it was actually like, and I had friends living over there, Pat and Mary Mulkerins. Mary had originally come from Ederney in County Fermanagh, and we said we would come up to visit them for a day when we arrived. I had met Pat in Paddy Mimnagh's house when we used to play cards, and Mena knew Mary already. Pat had told me one night to give him a call if I ever made it over to Scotland, and that's what I did, but I hadn't planned on spending my whole honeymoon with them.

We did manage to get to Edinburgh for one day and we both loved it, but we were having such a good time in Paisley that we stayed on for the whole two weeks. It turned out to be one of the best holidays of our lives. I finished up my honeymoon at a Rangers/Celtic match in Parkhead, playing a game of soccer against the Glasgow police, of all things. I got a lot of stick at that game, with some of the police screaming at me that I was 'a dirty Irish bastard', but sure we just laughed it all off. Mena meanwhile was off shopping and spending all the money.

When we got back home, we stacked all the wedding presents up in my parents' house and went to live in a caravan on a piece of land that my father had bought not far from Drumquin, about a mile and a half out on the Baronscourt Road. My parents had decided to build their own house on this site and move out of the family home, a council house in McCrea Park, so instead of us moving into the house with them still in it, we agreed to just move into the caravan.

We had already spoken to the Council about taking over the house when they moved on, with a view to eventually buying it when we could afford to, and that's exactly what we did years later. But we really enjoyed our few months of early married life in the caravan, having to go to the toilet out in the field, using a bucket at night, and cuddling up when it got freezing cold. I remember getting up on cold winter mornings when the condensation would be dripping down on our heads from the roof. Even though it didn't seem like it at the time, it was a great experience and made us grateful for what we had later in life.

Most of the younger generation don't understand what it was like years ago when money was really tight. They would laugh if you told them some of the ways we had to scrimp and save, but we really enjoyed our time in that wee caravan and it made us appreciate even more what we had when we eventually moved into the house.

When we first got married, Mena was working for a company called Desmond's in Irvinestown. I used to drive her every morning from Drumquin to Irvinestown, a good few miles, and then I'd have to drive on to Castlefin where I was working. It was a very early start for both of us and after a while we knew that we had to change something, so she applied for a job in the T&F, as we called the Tyrone and Fermanagh County Hospital. She became a cleaning lady there and she loved it. It was a psychiatric hospital and she made some great friends there, both with staff and with some of the patients. But then she got a chance of a job as a machinist in a branch of Desmond's in Omagh, which was much handier, because it was basically on our doorstep, so she gave up the cleaning job and went to work in the factory. This company made clothes for a number of companies, including Marks & Spencer and Dunnes Stores.

This was a grand job for Mena, and my mother had always said that if Mena ever got pregnant she would mind the baby for us as it would allow Mena to continue to work and bring in a few pounds. In fairness to my mother, she was great when our firstborn, Paula, came into the world. Mena was fine going back to work and, apart from obviously missing our baby, she seemed to manage really well. But when Ray came along we knew that it would be harder for my mother to cope with two babies. Mena was on maternity leave and, after having a chat about all our options, my mother said she's give it a try and see how she'd get on with the two of them. But just as Mena was preparing herself to go back to work, she fell pregnant with Tracey. There were just ten months between the two of them, so going back to working outside of the house was simply impossible.

Then, lo and behold, Shauna arrived and things got even

harder financially for us, but we knew there was no way Mena could leave the kids at home with a childminder or with my mother because it just wouldn't have worked. So she made the decision to stay at home and take care of everyone. She was run off her feet with the lot of them.

We were living in McCrea Park when Ray, our second child, came into the world on 8 December 1981. On the day Mena went into labour, I went straight down to my mother's house to stay with them. My parents have always been there for us over the years and their home is open to all of the family, all year round. I don't know what I would do without them in my life. But this particular time, they minded Paula for us as we awaited the arrival of baby number two, and I moved my stuff to their home so we were all under the one roof.

Back in those days, when kids were born, the father was never allowed to be around for the birth. When the mother was taken into hospital, the father disappeared and you'd ring the next morning to find out whether you had a son or a daughter. The labour room was seen as a place solely for the mother, the midwives, nurses, etc., and God forbid a father even come near the door or he'd be sent packing. It was good Catholic Ireland and a man knew his place at that time. So I never got to see any of my children with Mena come into this world. It is something that I really regret.

I have strong memories myself of when my own mother would disappear when I was a child. We would be shipped off to our grandmother's house and my father would have to wait outside the door of the bedroom until the baby arrived. When we were brought home, there'd be a new baby there and we were told that the stork had brought it, and sure we believed it. As a man you don't know what a woman has to go through when they give birth unless you are actually standing there beside them and see firsthand how difficult it is and how tiring it is. I think if men years ago knew what their wives were going through in childbirth there wouldn't have been ten or twelve kids in a family, which was the norm back then.

Ray was born in Tyrone County Hospital, as was our first baby Paula, and I remember how that winter was one of the bitterest I've ever experienced. On the day after he arrived into the world, I went back up to the house to get it ready for Mena and the new baby coming home but when I opened the front door the water met me coming down the stairs. Everything in the kitchen, the sitting-room, the landing, was destroyed. I could not believe it. It couldn't have happened at a worse time. And to top it all, I had no house insurance. I did my best to clear it up, but the damage was huge.

It turned out that a pipe had burst and the Council decided that it wasn't their responsibility. My parents lent us the money to get it sorted, and meanwhile Ray and Mena spent the first few weeks after his birth in my parents' house along with young Paula. Every mother likes to take her baby back home and have all the neighbours and friends in to see the new arrival, but we had no choice but to stay out of the house until it was all sorted and habitable again. We were out of the house for a couple of weeks, but we just got on with it because there was nothing we could do to change it.

We had always had trouble in the house with an unusual smell, which would get worse at certain times of the year. We could never make out where it was coming from or what was causing it. Then one night, when we were about five or six years married, Mena went upstairs and found the bedroom filled with smoke. We got onto the housing executive and they came out and did a smoke test on the chimney, but they could find nothing wrong. The problem continued and we got them out again, and this time they realized that we had a big problem. There was only one flue for both our house and the house next door. We were lucky that there had never been a fire or both families could have been wiped out. At that time, we had three children, Paula, Raymond and Tracey. It was too much of a risk for everyone to stay on while they were carrying out the work, so they had to evacuate us out of the house and we had to live in a caravan on the street. Looking back it was quite funny and, despite the cramped conditions, we all got on with things. We were very grateful for our little house when we eventually moved back in.

But we had many a good time – a lot more good than bad – and the children absolutely loved the area and had loads of friends. It was one of those close-knit communities that'd be hard to find anywhere in Ireland today. If you were stuck for a bit of butter or a pint of milk, you only had to ask the next-door neighbour, and when they were stuck for something they knew that they could knock into you. It's something that has gone by the wayside in housing estates all over Ireland and Northern Ireland nowadays and it's a huge loss. Today you would be lucky if you knew your next-door neighbour's surname, never mind what they worked at. People nowadays are only concerned with themselves and how much money they have in their bank accounts and it's a big shame.

We had very little money growing up as kids, and when Mena and I were raising our own children we had very few luxuries, but what we had we appreciated and the kids never wanted for anything. They valued what they had and knew that we were giving them as much as we could. My biggest regret, though, to this day is that I couldn't have provided more for Mena when she was alive because she was a true lady in every sense of the word and she deserved the best. She did a great job bringing up our family and she was a huge loss in our lives when she was taken from us.

The only real break Mena got from the mania in our house was when there was a football match on, because they all loved football. When I'd be refereeing a game, I'd take them all along with me. Shauna was a Tyrone supporter through and through. When there was a GAA match on between Fermanagh and Tyrone, the tension in the house was mad. Mena was a Fermanagh supporter and the rest of us were all up for our home county. It wouldn't mean much to people who don't support Gaelic football, but the game was our life. Back in 2003, when Tyrone met Fermanagh in the All-Ireland quarter-finals, we all said that we would have loved to have had Mena there for the game because she would have been slagged off, left, right and centre. Mena didn't give a damn about football but she loved to stir things with Shauna because she knew how much Shauna loved the game.

In some parts of Ireland and Northern Ireland, Gaelic football is truly a passion and we are one of those families who plan everything around a Tyrone game. It's the adrenalin rush that you get from it that spurs you on. There is simply nothing like being at a GAA match for the whole atmosphere and the craic, and we always think of Mena when there's a big game on.

Mena loved nothing more than to sit at home and knit, and

she was a fantastic Aran knitter. She was truly gifted. Her own mother was also an Aran knitter, but she couldn't hold a candle to Mena. She knitted for a well-known shop called Magees in Donegal, where everyone up north went to buy a good Aran sweater. It was hugely popular with the tourists as well, and I'd say to this day there are people in America and Canada who have sweaters knitted by Mena.

She may be gone, but I am sure there are still many sweaters around that were knitted with her very own hands.

It wasn't a job to her. She was so relaxed with a pair of knitting needles in her hands. She'd sit there knitting away and reading a Catherine Cookson novel at the same time, and she'd be totally chilled out. We had a wee room off the kitchen at the back of the house and it was full to the roof with wool. Mena would buy wool everywhere she went, in every colour. She had orders all year round and she knitted steadily from August until December for one particular woman who placed her order every summer for her grandchildren's Christmas jumpers. Everyone knew of Mena for her knitting skills. People knew that if they ordered off Mena they'd have a quality garment that would last years. She was very proud of her work. I'd be invited to football dinner dances and darts dinner dances and she wouldn't be interested in any of them. She'd tell me to head off and she'd stay at home with the kids and knit. The family was her life and her knitting kept her busy. She was like that from the day we got married.

She started at home when we were only a few years married and she'd be minding the children. She always looked after our own kids and then she began minding my brother's children and then a neighbour's kids. Looking after youngsters, whether they'd be her own or someone else's, never seemed to be a chore for Mena. She took everything in her stride. It was lucky that she was so placid because I was never at home back then and I'm sure the youngsters must have been a handful.

When they were very young I'd be away a lot of the time at referees' meetings or refereeing soccer games somewhere or playing darts. Mena basically ran the home single-handedly. Looking back at my life, it's one of the things I wish I could have changed, because I lost out on so much when the kids were growing up. But back then, most men worked day and night to bring in a few shillings to keep things going. And most of us went straight to the pub after work to wind down.

In fact, I stopped playing darts a few years after we got married because I was drinking too much at the matches. I took up football instead, but it meant that I'd be working all day and then at matches at night, or doing something related to football. Sport was my life and I loved being active and out in the air. Mena never really complained about me being out and about all the time. She just took it for granted that this was how I was and she got on with things. She probably secretly cursed me if the truth be known, but she never asked me not to go out in all our years of marriage.

She was a great mother, a strict mother but a very loving person all round. If the girls wanted to go to a disco on the Saturday night and Mena said no, then they'd come straight to their daddy, knowing I'd probably cave in and say yes. They knew they had me wrapped around their little fingers, but in fairness to Mena she always stood her ground.

As the kids came along, things got very tight and holidays were rare. We went a couple of times to a caravan site in

Ballintragh, County Mayo, and had a few trips around Done-gal, but that was the extent of it. Then in 1995, I left the Nestlé factory, where I had been working for more than 20 years. I worked for ten of those years as a labourer and I spent the other ten working on the production line where they made powdered milk, and I finished up in the stores. It was a sad day when I lost my job in Nestlé, as I had so many good memories and so many good friendships there. But we got by.

We spent my few bob from the redundancy on a family holiday to Lanzarote. It was our first foreign holiday as a family and we had a great time. It was an amazing break as the kids had never had the experience of being in hot sunny weather with a swimming pool and a beach on the doorstep. They had a ball.

Then in 1997, when the Halifax Building Society, where we had our mortgage, changed from being a building society to a bank, we cashed in about 160 shares. The price of shares had gone through the roof as everyone jumped on the bandwagon to get a piece of the pie, so we sold what we had and booked a holiday to Fuerteventura. It was a fantastic family holiday. Everyone enjoyed that break in the sun, and when we got home we got about our daily lives as usual and everything was going fine.

Little did any of us know just how soon that idyllic life would all come crashing down around us.

We went back to Lanzarote after Mena died. Tracey took me for my fiftieth birthday, just me, Tracey and Mark, her husband. It was very hard on us all to revisit some of the places we had all once gone to as a family. But we got on with things and made the most of it. As people say, and sometimes it seems callous to those affected, but life does have to go on. Hard as it may be, that's just the way it is.

Chapter 3

The Aftermath

The days and weeks that followed the attack were horrific for us all. People who weren't even directly affected by the bombing were walking around with a look of despair clearly etched on their faces. And for those of us who were affected, life just seemed pointless. It was as if there were no reason to go on any more. We had all lost so many loved ones, the funerals were still going on and people were still calling at the house. It was very difficult to cope.

Omagh was like a ghost town, and as if a cloud of gloom hung over everyone. Every single day we were faced with stories in the newspapers and on TV about the bombing and who could possibly have carried it out. We were watching interviews with families in the same position as ourselves, trying to come to terms with what had taken place. It was hard enough to cope with it as a family, but being faced with it every day in the media as well made it an awful lot worse.

Shauna was in hospital for a fortnight after Mena's funeral, and to be honest if she had not been there, alive and fighting, I would probably be dead. I wouldn't have lasted three days, never mind three weeks, if I had lost her as well that day. If I had found her under her mammy's body, that would have been it for me. Losing any of my children would have brought me to my knees. My own kids know that Shauna, being the baby, was always a daddy's girl, and I don't know what I would have done had God taken her from me as well.

The support from our neighbours and friends was fantastic. Everyone was praying for my little girl and we all hoped that she would be strong enough to cope with the horrific injuries she had sustained to her face that day, never mind having to cope with the fact that her mother wasn't there for her, to look after her when she needed it most. I had always known she was a little fighter but I could never have imagined just how strong she would actually be.

When Shauna got out of hospital, she refused to hide away. I don't know how bad her injuries really were on the day of the bombing, because she never allowed me to see her without a cover on her face, but I do know, from talking to the surgeons, that she had the most horrific tears in her skin. They had told me that that no matter how many operations or procedures she had, she would still have to cope with very bad scarring for the rest of her life. They had promised to do whatever they could to repair as much as possible, but they told us out straight that the marks would always be there. She would never for one minute be able to forget 15 August 1998, because for the rest of her life, every time she looked into a mirror, she would see the scars of what had happened that day.

She was to carry on with her treatment and have regular check-ups with the doctor in Derry who had carried out the operations. However, headstrong as ever, the meeting in his office just weeks later made it clear that Shauna was battling this on her own and in her own way, and no one could tell her otherwise. When he told her that she had two options – one, to wear a silicone sheet on her face to protect the wounds, encourage healing and cover the scars; or two, to wear a complete face mask – she responded by saying, 'Well, doctor, there's also a third option: wear nothing.' He was very surprised by the reply and asked her if she was not concerned about the future and how she'd cope with boyfriends. Her answer to that was, 'If they don't like me the way I am, then tough.' She walked out of that doctor's room that day, determined that she would face life as she was, and no one could convince her otherwise. And she has been that strong-willed ever since.

Throughout all of this, poor Paula was anxiously waiting on news to see if she had been accepted into University College Belfast, but I knew she was having reservations. She said to me one day that she felt it might be better if she took a year out. I knew that she only wanted to do that because she was worried about leaving me and the other children, because she would have had to move out if she got a university place. But I didn't want her to put her life on hold and, as they say, a bad situation can bring good things at times.

A lady called Ruth Blair came down to visit Paula a few days after the funeral. She had lost a member of her own family in the Enniskillen bombing and she had taught Paula in the technical college in Enniskillen. She asked her if she had heard anything from the college, and when Paula said that she hadn't, she told her that she would probably get word in the coming days. I'm sure that woman took things into her own hands, because a week later Paula got the letter offering her a place at Stranmillis University College in Belfast to study teaching. We were all delighted for her, but we knew it would be hard getting used to not having her around as well.

Once again, Paula said that she wasn't sure about what to do and she was still playing with the idea of taking a year out. But I told her straight out that she would do no such thing. She would go to Belfast and if she didn't like it then there was a bus that left every hour or so and she could come back home, but she had to take the opportunity and see how she got on. Thank God she went. At the start she would phone me three or four times a day, but thankfully, as time went on, it went to once a day and then eventually she'd ring once a week.

We missed Paula around the house, but I didn't want her putting her life on hold for me and I knew Mena wouldn't have wanted that either. She stuck it out and she eventually qualified as a teacher. I was so proud of her, because it's hard enough for a child to leave home in normal circumstances and to move to a strange place where she knows nobody, but after all she had been through, it was a miracle she did so well. She was also reading the news stories about Omagh and who was believed to be responsible for it every single day for months after and she had to deal with that as well, all on her own. But somehow she managed to get through it.

All of the kids were fantastic. It was very difficult for them not having their mother around and I was of no help whatso-ever, because basically I just crumbled. To be perfectly honest, they had no father back then. My days and nights were taken up with drink. I'd get up in the morning and all I wanted to do was to go to the pub.

At the start, in the very early days, I would hang on until the evening and then come home in an awful state in the early hours of the morning. The pub became an escape route for me out of the house because everywhere I looked there were memories of Mena. She loved her home, and everything in the house was chosen by her: furniture, cushions, curtains, pictures, everything. Our bedroom still smelt of her perfume. Her clothes were still in the wardrobe. Things she had left lying around were still in the places she'd put them. I didn't want to move anything because she had touched them.

I felt Mena everywhere. I knew that she was still around, watching over us. I never felt scared, more comforted, but also devastated, because if she was there, I just wanted to see her, talk to her. I missed her so much. It killed me to know she was there but I couldn't see her. I talked to her all the time as I pottered around on my own. I told her how I felt, how I missed her. I couldn't tell the kids how I felt; I didn't want them to think that I was going mad. But there were things happening around the house all the time and in my heart I knew that it was Mena's spirit still around us. There were times when I would turn off the television and leave the room and by the time I came back in, the TV would be back on and there would be no one around; this was a regular occurrence.

I had my own little armchair in the kitchen and that's where I would spend most of my time, just sitting there with my cockatiel on my shoulder and our little Jack Russell dog, Patch, at my feet or on my lap. Many a time as I sat there, the kettle would boil of its own accord and switch off or the washing machine would just switch on. A lot of electrical things in the house just seemed to get a mind of their own after Mena died. There was never anything unusual in the house before her death; it all began within a couple of weeks after we buried her.

At first, I honestly thought that my mind was playing tricks on me at times or that maybe we had a genuine problem with the electrics. Most of the occurrences would take place when I was sober, so I couldn't really blame the drink. It happened so often that I just kind of accepted that this was the way it was going to be. But even though I knew that I wasn't imagining it, I still doubted what I was seeing and hearing.

Then one day when the girls were there we started to talk about different things and how we were all feeling, and out of the blue the subject came up. I could not believe it when the girls said that similar things had been happening to them. I didn't bring it up, they did, but it was a comfort to me knowing that it wasn't just me imagining things.

The girls said that things were being moved about in their bedrooms all the time. Clothes that were put in one place would end up somewhere else. They all had the same feeling as me, as if they were being watched over. In fact, on one occasion the girls came into the room to find that all of the clothes they had left on the floor were out in the back garden, as if someone had picked them all up and flung them out of the window. It sounds mad even saying it, but it happened.

The odd thing was that Mena used to get so frustrated with them for throwing their clothes on the bedroom floor that, when she really lost it, she would threaten to throw the clothes out the window. So the day they came in to find their stuff in the back yard really made them sit up and think. Just like me, though, none of them was scared. It was as if we all knew that it was just Mena keeping a watchful eye over us all. We used to joke and say that she was making sure we didn't let the place fall apart.

I gradually got used to everything happening, but I had a very unusual experience one day in our home that will always stick in my mind, because it was totally inexplicable. We had tried to make excuses or come up with reasons for certain things that were going on, but this was different. I did a lot of work at the time for the St Vincent de Paul Society, and people knew where I lived so they often called directly to the house. On this particular day I was absolutely wrecked because there seemed to be people knocking at the door all day for one thing or another, so I decided to put the lock on the door and just sit down on my own and relax for a while. I made myself a cup of tea and decided that whoever knocked, whether I knew them or not, I wasn't going to answer. I just needed some time to myself. So that's what I did and I sat there watching the snooker on the TV.

After a bit of time I heard the front door open and someone come in, close the door and walk up the stairs. Forgetting it was locked from the inside, I immediately thought that it was Ray and that he'd gone straight up to his room. But then it dawned on me that there was no way he could have got in. So I got up, walked to the end of the stairs and called up to him. There was no answer, so I headed up the stairs and checked every single room. Nothing; no one was there. A shiver went down my spine and I knew that what had happened just could not be explained. I had clearly heard the door open and close and I clearly heard the footsteps going up the stairs.

All I could do at times like that was to say a prayer for my wife and carry on as if nothing had happened. Up until the time when the rest of them told me about what was happening to them, I had to try to be strong for everyone else and not let them see me falling apart.

I often wondered why Ray wouldn't stay in the house on his own, and it was only when all of this came out that I realized why: he was having the same experiences as the rest of us and he never said a thing. Ray is different to the girls. He comes and goes and does his own thing, and he was dealing with his grief in his own way. He was never a one for talking about how he felt and we knew just to let him deal with his own feelings himself. He knew that we were there if he ever needed us. Everyone deals with loss in their own way, but we all knew that losing his mother affected him greatly. He just wasn't one for wearing his heart on his sleeve.

Around this time, my mother Maggie was in the house a lot. She was always around when Mena was alive, and she'd clean the place and give her a hand with whatever needed doing. Mena would just let her and she'd be delighted with the help. The only person Mena was happy leaving the children with was my mother; she trusted her completely. The two of them always had a very close bond. So, after Mena died, my mother was there all the time, cooking and cleaning and making sure that we were all OK. When we'd come in every evening, my mother would have dinner ready and the house would be spotless. But she really missed having Mena around for company.

When everything started coming out about the strange things that were happening around the house, my mother shocked us all. She told us that she hadn't said anything to us before this because she didn't want to upset us, but she had been cleaning the rooms upstairs one day when, all of a sudden, she saw a vision of Mena standing in front of her, having come out of the bathroom. My mother just stood still and

Mena simply smiled at her, said nothing and disappeared. She is convinced that it was Mena, and said her body shape was kind of blurred, but she looked very happy. She couldn't say what she was wearing or anything like that, just that she was a blurry shape surrounded in a white light and she looked radiant. It gave my mother a feeling of inner peace and she believed that Mena was letting her know that she was happy to see her in the house, helping us all get through things. She never saw her again but she always felt that she was around her, looking over her. Knowing that my own mother had experienced something as well made me feel a bit better, because there is no way in the world that my mother would make something like that up.

As the months went on, my comfort at knowing Mena was around changed to concern. It became a big burden, because I started to worry about whether or not Mena was happy, and if she *was* happy, then why had her spirit not moved on? It was an unusual situation for us all, because in one way we were at peace knowing that she was with us. I would have given anything at the time to have seen her in front of me, smiling, like she did for my mother. On the other hand, we were also concerned that she mightn't be at rest.

It started to play on my mind quite a lot, and one day I had a chat with the children. We decided that we would ask Father Mullen, who was in our parish at that stage, if he would come and bless the house for us. I was never a very religious person – Mena was – but I wanted the priest to come to the house and say a prayer for her. It just felt like it was the right thing to do, and I knew that Mena would have been happy knowing that I was happy bringing a priest in to say a few prayers. Father Mullen came and said a few prayers for Mena and blessed each room with holy water. He told me at the time that Mena was only there to watch over us and we had nothing to fear, but we explained to him that none of us feared anything anyway. After he left we were all at ease; totally relaxed, and we all just hoped that Mena was happy.

Despite the air of calmness from the rest of us in the family, there was no let-up in the unusual activity and we finally all just accepted that Mena would only stay around us until she felt that she was ready to go herself. The various things that were taking place gave us comfort to some extent, because we knew that although we couldn't see her, she was there, all the time, and we were still being cared for.

We tried as best we could to get on with our lives, but I was falling apart bit by bit. Looking back, I realize that I never really spoke to my children about how they felt, not the way I should have. It was very selfish of me as a father, but I was just wallowing in my own self-pity. I never noticed how everyone else was doing, nor did I really care.

I hadn't gone back to work, and although they kept my job open for me for a long time, they eventually realized that I wasn't heading back anytime soon. One day they sent someone around to collect the keys to the truck, and it was driven back to the depot. I watched it being driven away and I never had a second thought about what would happen next, how the future would pan out.

At that time I never even thought about how we would all get by without my wage coming in. It never dawned on me how hard it would be, money-wise, to keep going. All I cared about was alcohol and whether I had enough money in my pocket to buy a few pints and a few shorts.

I had basically started on a downward drinking spiral within weeks of losing my wife. And by this time, my drinking habit had escalated totally out of control. It had gone from going out at night to going out first thing in the morning for 'the hair of the dog' – 'a curer'. It got to the stage where I felt that I wouldn't be able to function if I didn't go straight to the pub once it opened. I would drink a lorry-load of beer and then have a few brandies on the side, and by the time the place closed I would be nearly falling home.

On some occasions I'd get into my car and drive home absolutely drunk. I wouldn't have been able to see in front of me and yet I'd get behind that wheel, not thinking of myself, my children or any other poor innocent person on the road.

This went on for three or four years. I could see that my children were upset at how I was carrying on but I didn't care how anyone else felt; I was 'coping' with everything in my own way, and that way just happened to be by drinking myself into a drunken stupor. It's not something I'm at all proud of, but it's the truth.

I would be gone all day, maybe calling at my mother's house for a bite to eat at some stage and then back to the pub until I fell out of it. There were times when I wouldn't have seen the children for days on end because I would get home so late that I would just about crawl up the stairs and fall into bed. My mother was on my back all the time. She was terrified for the kids and terrified for me. She could see me falling apart – every dog on the street could see how bad I was – but in my head there was no way back. I had lost everything the day I lost Mena and I just wasn't coping. Looking back on my worst days, I have to say I wouldn't have got by without my mother beside me. If there were medals for best parenting, she would have won them all. I am so grateful that she is still here with me to this day.

Shauna was also on at me all the time to stop drinking and get some professional help, but I wasn't into it at all. Just to get her off my back, I agreed to go to talk to someone about the grieving process, because the children were going to someone already and they felt it was helping them. But I went to one session in the early days and that was that. To be honest, I had made my mind up before I had even gone to see the counsellor that day that there was no way I was going back. I couldn't see any point in telling some complete stranger how I was feeling and what I was doing. The poor counsellor knew from the out-set that I wasn't there of my own free will, and although I said I would come back for another session, I think he knew in his own heart that he'd probably never see me again. I wasn't ready to deal with things, and that was that.

Of course, things only got worse, and the drinking and the chain-smoking continued. I was smoking up to 100 cigarettes a day at that stage and my chest was in bits. I had an awful cough and my breathing was very bad. I couldn't walk a few hundred yards without going into a fit of coughing, but I didn't care about my health at all. As far as I was concerned, if God took me, then he took me, because I was of no use to anyone on Earth as it was.

Over the years I listened to the girls nagging at me and, just to keep them happy, I went to counselling on and off as part of the Omagh survivors' group, but it still never appealed to me at the time and I couldn't understand what these fami-lies were getting out of talking about their problems in front of everyone, total strangers really. Because I wasn't comfortable with the whole format I didn't go to too many of these sessions, so they were of no benefit to me at all. I only went because everyone else was going as part of the group and I felt that if I didn't go with them I was letting other people down. It was a waste of time for me back then, so I gave up on them after a while. I chose to battle on myself, alone.

I suppose I always thought that I could do it myself and that one day I would wake up and it would all be grand. But it doesn't happen like that. It just takes a long time for you to realize it. But I always felt, back then – and I still feel the same to this day – that you can only help yourself at the end of it all. If you are not ready to move on, there is nothing in this world that can make you. But I will admit that there are times when you need a bit of a shove to make you realize that something has to be done, and sometimes outside help is needed. Drink only numbs you for a certain amount of time, and pills just put everything into a little compartment until they start wearing off. Then all your problems come back again and hit you twice as hard. It is a vicious circle.

There were times back then when I would sit in my chair in the kitchen and look around and realize that, really, I was on my own. Yes, I still had Shauna and Ray living with me, but the house always seemed to be empty. The two older girls were now at university: Tracey had gone off to drama school in Belfast about a year after the bombing. I was delighted that she was finally moving on, but I missed her around the house. I also knew that soon the other two would be gone, and then what? I'd be left with an empty house with nothing but the sound of a clock ticking. What would I do with my life then?

I had been bottling everything up inside me for so long and it was doing me no good. I was getting deeper and deeper into a black mood. I'd go down to my mother, who was always giving me grief about drinking, even if I hadn't been drinking at all that day, but I'd act as if I was fine and everything was grand. Once I'd had a cup of tea and she'd stopped nagging, I'd head home, sit in the armchair as usual and just want to die.

The house was empty and I couldn't cope with it at all. Mena was such a home bird and she was always there for me. It just didn't feel right not having her around. I would often sit there and ask God: why Mena and not me? Why did he have to take her that day? Mena would have been better left on Earth to mind the children; she would have been much stronger than me. There's no way she would have drunk herself into a stupor, feeling sorry for herself.

I had a double-barrelled shotgun upstairs from years earlier when I used to head off shooting rabbits in the fields; it was a Kestrel, and I hadn't used it for a long time, since well before Mena died. One night I came in from the pub feeling very depressed. I went upstairs and, without anyone knowing, I took it down and sat on the chair in the kitchen, with the gun cocked between my legs and the barrel aimed at my face. I tried to build up the courage to pull the trigger and end it all. I was so low that I thought everyone would be better off without me. In my mind, if I was gone they could all move on and make a better life for themselves, because I was only making things worse for everyone around me – my children, my parents, my friends, everyone. I felt I had no purpose in life and nothing left to live for. I sat there for ages that first night, contemplating pulling that trigger, knowing that if I just built up the courage to do it I could end all this nightmare in a matter of seconds, and I would be free.

I tried this three times over the years, trying to build up the courage each and every time to just do it, just pull that trigger. But each and every time, something would catch my eye in the room, like a photo of Mena or a picture of the kids, and I'd panic and back down.

I never told anyone about those times for years because, in my mind, it was only a matter of 'when', not 'if'. I always told myself that one way or another the day would come when I would finish it all. I didn't want anyone to stop me once I had decided to go ahead and do it. Knowing the shotgun was there was a comfort to me because, once it was within my grasp, I knew I had a way out if things got too much for me. It had been lying there unused for years, but it was clean and it would have done the job.

Then, after months of further depression and further planning to end it all, I woke up one morning, having had the gun out the night before, and I decided there and then to get it out of the house once and for all, just in case I did eventually crack. I don't know why I decided to stop planning my own death, but I did. So that morning I went up to the local police station and handed in my permit. I then went to the gun shop where I had bought the shotgun, and simply handed it back to the owner. I could have sold it back to him or put it in the local paper or on the Internet, but I didn't want a penny for it. I just wanted it out of the way so I couldn't use it.

When I walked away from the shop that day, I didn't know whether I was happy or sad, because having the gun in the house had genuinely been like a comfort blanket to me all that time. But on the other hand, for the sake of my children, I knew it was the right thing to do.

I was constantly dealing with guilt, asking myself the same questions over and over again: Why did I take Mena into Omagh that day? Why did I leave her and go into another shop? It's very hard to accept this, but I eventually realized that she was destined to be killed that day. It sounds very harsh, but it didn't matter where I was – she was going to die that day and I couldn't have stopped it. It was the same for every single person who lost their lives that day. I believe now that all our lives are mapped out for us from the day we are born. It is simply fate working when things go right or wrong. We have absolutely no control over it. It just took me a long time to accept that.

As the weeks and months went on, everyone tried their best to get me out of the spiralling depression I was in. The doctor even gave me some tablets to take that he said would help to relax me so that I could at least get some sleep. I took them for a few weeks, finished off the course he had prescribed and then, after a while, I just didn't bother getting the prescription renewed. Looking back on things now, it was as if I didn't want anything to work. In a way I was happy the way I was because I didn't want to be 'cured'.

Mena's family meant everything to her and she lived for the children; they were her life. And I knew in my heart that she would have been distraught if she had seen how things were going back home. She would have been furious with me for not taking control of things, for falling apart at the seams. She would have expected a lot more of me. But unfortunately, in my mind there was nothing I could do to make things better, and that was just how it was. I found it hard to see a way out of it all.

Try as I might to put things behind me after the bombing, the hatred was always there. Over the years the bitterness I felt for those responsible began to eat me up, consume me. All I wanted was to see those responsible brought to court, to see their faces and hear the sentence handed out for taking the lives of 31 people, including unborn twins.

The memories of what happened that day are still firmly etched on my mind, and I know they will never leave me. It has been hard to cope with through the years.

The cemetery where Mena was buried was just a stone's throw from the house in McCrea Park and so, when I got up in the morning and pulled back the curtains, the first thing I would see was Mena's grave, and it was the last thing I would see before I went to bed at night. Each night I would watch the everlasting candle we had placed on the headstone flickering in the wind, as if her spirit were there, waiting on us to look out to let us know that she was still around, watching over us.

Comforting though this may have been, it was also very hard for us all to have to face this each and every day. There was no escaping it at all. Mena was in our hearts all the time, but it's not very helpful to stare at your wife's or your mother's grave every single day, all the time. It's just a constant reminder that she is dead and that the only thing you will ever see of her for the rest of your life is her grave. You can't move on fully because you feel guilty about moving on, knowing the person is so near you, but not really there at all. The sight of a grave is not a very positive image, and I think being able to see her headstone and the candle on the grave all the time when we were at home wasn't helping things and made the grieving process so much harder. Even when I went to the pub, I had to face the grave-yard on my way back, so escaping to the pub was a lost cause at the end of the night, because you were hit with reality once again walking back home.

So, after having a chat with the rest of the family, I made a very hard decision: to put the family home up for sale. My parents were fine with this, and so were my brothers and sister. The house had been in the family since the 1970s but I knew it was time for me to move on.

Unfortunately, once we'd put it on the market, no one seemed to be biting at all. Then one of my brothers said that he would be interested in buying it himself. I was delighted, because it made things a lot easier for everyone if I sold it within the family, with no estate agent's fees and our family home still in the family. We struck a deal between us that we were both happy with, and I set about packing for the big move.

It was a very difficult job. Not only did we have to leave behind all the memories of the kids growing up, the birthday parties, the laughter and the tears, but we also had to accept that we were essentially leaving behind a part of our lives when Mena was around, fussing about the kitchen, cleaning up after every-one, knitting her Aran sweaters. It was a huge upheaval for every-one, both physically and emotionally. When it came to packing everything away, the memories came flooding back so many times. We would find an item of clothing belonging to Mena or an ornament or a present that she might have bought the kids when they were younger. It was heartbreaking for everyone.

Each of us had our own memories and heartaches associated with McCrea Park. There was many a time during the move that we all shed a tear or two. Even though I knew we would be back in the house for many years to come, visiting my brother and his family, it was still very hard when I finally closed that door behind me and drove off with all of our belongings. I thought of all the things we had saved for, bought and treasured as a family over the years. But we all did our best to stay strong through it all.

The fact that the house was still in the family was a huge help, I believe. It would probably have been an awful lot harder for the kids to move on, especially if they had to drive by the house in the future and see other people living there, in their family home. But despite the sense of loss, I was genuinely looking forward to moving on. In my mind I wasn't leaving Mena behind; I was trying to move us forward as a family.

That was in July of 2004. That day, we moved to a lovely bungalow on Creaghmore Road in Drumquin, just a few miles from our old house. It was a bigger house altogether. It was a four-bedroomed bungalow, much larger and more modern than our three-bedroomed two-storey house.

However, despite the big space and the lovely garden, I was never happy in it; I just couldn't settle. I had spent 34 years of my life in McCrea Park, and I just couldn't settle into this new place at all. I didn't even go to the local pubs. I never felt that it was a place I could call home. I went for a few drinks a couple of times with Shauna before she went away to live and work in Australia, but I never really found a pub that I could have called my 'local'. It never lived up to what I'd had where we used to live.

No matter how hard I tried to make the new house a home, I couldn't feel the same in it at all. I didn't feel when I went to bed that I was actually going to bed. Walking up a hallway to get to the bedroom instead of walking up a staircase just didn't feel right. I had climbed those stairs for so many years in Drumquin, and when I got to the top I always felt like I was just minutes away from a good night's sleep. But walking up that hallway felt like I could have been simply going into any other room in the house. To me, when you went to bed you went 'up to bed', and that wasn't the case in Creaghmore.

But I was glad that I had done it, that I took that gamble. It was the first break I had made since the bombing. I remember one man saying to me at the time that he couldn't understand why I had left it so long to get out of McCrea Park. He was probably right; maybe I should have moved out sooner, but I went when I felt it was right to go. I had to make sure that the children all felt the same as me, because they had spent all of their lives in our cosy little three-bed home and to them it was a place where they felt their mammy was. The move would never have taken place if they had been against it.

I liked the area itself and the people were very friendly, but it just wasn't the right place for me. It's hard when you are used to living in one area for so long to make that upheaval, and I think it was even harder for me as a widower because I didn't have Mena around to make a proper home of it. She would probably have settled in quite quickly, put the finishing homely touches to it and everything would have been fine, but without her it was a struggle.

We could all still feel her presence around us and things were happening in this house that had happened in McCrea Park, so it was quite obvious from very early on that Mena hadn't stayed on back in the old house. As far as we could see, wherever we were going, Mena was going too. In a way it was a comfort to us knowing that she was still around, taking care of us, and that she didn't feel we were abandoning her spirit to move on without her.

The same problems we'd encountered with electrical items working of their own accord in our first house continued in the new house, too. The washing machine would start up without anyone turning it on; the kettle would boil and switch off when no one was about; and things would move about the place.

In my mind Mena was letting us know all the time that she was still with us and that it didn't matter where we went, she'd follow us until she felt it was time to move on. But I believe in my heart that she wasn't happy in the new house either, and as far as the whole family was concerned, the new life we were hoping to start just wasn't meant to start there.

So I made my mind up to see what the interest would be like if I put the bungalow up for sale. I was very surprised by how many people actually wanted, unlike me, to live in a bungalow. We had a lot of interest very quickly and a lot of people came to view it. As the interest grew, the price went up and up. It didn't take long for me to realize that I wouldn't have a problem selling it. So I started looking for another house immediately, because it became fairly obvious that a sale would go through very quickly if I was serious about moving. So I started once again hunting for a new place to call home, a place where I could, once again, try to rebuild my life.

I was dealing with a local auctioneer who had secured a good offer for our house, but the house that I wanted to buy seemed to be getting more interest than usual as far as this auctioneer was concerned and the price was escalating way beyond the norm. Every other day I was getting a call saying that the price had gone up again as there was another 'interested party'. Then one day I just got sick of it all and when he rang to say it had gone up by yet another thousand pounds, I told him to stick it.

I just wanted a nice home where I could happily settle in and get on with things again. He told me that I had now created a situation whereby he had two unhappy bidders – the one looking to buy my house, and me. I put the phone down on that man that day and I just thought that everything happens for a reason, and that for some reason I was not meant to move into that house. I knew that in time I would get the house I was meant to get. And I did.

Just weeks later I got a call from a man whom, as far as I knew, I had never met before. He told me that his house was up for sale and he had heard that I was interested in getting a house in his area, Kevlin, and he was very interested in my home. We arranged to meet up and have a chat. He said that he knew my house was worth a bit more than his own because of the area it was in and the fact that it was a bungalow, but that if I was interested, we could possibly do a swap and he would give me a few bob extra for my home.

I went to see his house. When I got talking to him, he asked me if I remembered him. His name was Gary Mullen. I thought that I had never set eyes on the man in my life before that day, but he told me that he knew who I was – for he was the man whose mobile phone I had grabbed on the day of the Omagh bombing, as I ran down the street, so that I could ring my father to tell him that Mena was dead.

It was a very unusual experience listening to his version of things. We had a good chat about what happened on that day.

We both had horrific memories. He hadn't lost anyone in the bombing but he understood how I felt because he was there on the day and he saw first-hand the devastation that was caused.

Gary came and saw my home after that and, although I was keen to move to Kevlin, I was still a bit unsure, so I told him that I would have to pass on the deal until I was sure of what I wanted. Ray and Shauna loved our old house and although they weren't mad about the new bungalow they weren't that pushed about moving again; but then, just weeks later, Shauna decided to move out of Creaghmore and into her own place. I decided, with Shauna moving on, that the right thing for me to do would be to take up the offer of the house in Kevlin. So I rang Gary back, arranged to meet and we shook hands on a deal. He was delighted; we both were.

Once again, then, we packed up and were on the move. It was amazing how, for more than 30 years, we had lived in the one little cosy house and suddenly, within a year, we had moved twice. I don't know if I was trying to run away from things – maybe I was – but I knew that I wouldn't have been able to settle down anywhere until I felt happy and relaxed. I was sure that once I moved back nearer to our original home, I would be fine. And I was.

Being back in the familiar setting of an upstairs/downstairs house felt normal again and I finally felt that I was content. The kids all liked the house as well. It would never be McCrea Park and they would never have their mammy back, but I think they were happy for me because they knew that I was much more comfortable in this house. In fairness, they just wanted me to be happy. I think Ray would have been fine wherever we moved. He just wanted to be able to come in from the pub after a night out with his pals and lie his head down, but he did seem happy as well when we made that move.

The neighbours were all very welcoming; most of them knew of me because of the bombing and they all welcomed us into the area with open arms. So we started to get on with our lives again and we set about redecorating and putting our own touches to our new home. I finally felt as if this was where we were meant to be.

We couldn't turn back time – we all knew that – but we had made a start at moving on. In the months and years that followed, I spoke to the press off and on in relation to the bombing, as they wanted to know how families were coping and how we felt about the delays in arresting those responsible. Shauna didn't like me giving interviews because it upset her every time it was brought up. It drew unwanted attention to her again. But that was how I dealt with things and I didn't want the world to forget what had happened.

It hadn't been easy for Paula and Tracey as the two older girls, because all of the focus was on Shauna at the time, since she was physically injured. What I didn't realize was that I was giving all the attention, as usual, to the youngest and I forgot that the other kids, including Ray, had all gone through their own trauma and that they would be mentally scarred for the rest of their lives as well. As my mother once said, Shauna could march me up the road, stand me on a stool, put a rope around my neck and kick the stool over, and I wouldn't say a thing. I suppose that was because she was my baby, I always felt I had to protect her.

But when the other girls left home, Shauna was the one left to put up with me and my drunken nights, and she had a hell of a lot to put up with. I would head off to Tom O'Kane's pub most nights and I wouldn't come home until I had no choice because I couldn't stand. I remember going down there one St Patrick's Day morning and coming home at 2:00 p.m., absolutely drunk. I went to bed, got back up at 7:00 p.m. and headed off again for more drink, falling in the door at whatever hour of the morning it was. I would down a pint of beer in two mouthfuls and order another. I'd have the brandy chaser lined up already on the side, to knock back straight after the pint. And I had let my child witness this most nights of the week and simply expected her to take it or leave it. Back then, it never once dawned on me that she was still a child and I was supposedly the father, the guardian, there to care for her.

It wasn't a life at all. For me it was just an existence and for the kids, I suppose, it was a nightmare. I'd go from one day to the next drinking, sleeping and drinking and I could see no way back. The only break I'd have was a bit of dinner at my mother's at some stage during the day. If I'm to be honest with myself, I probably didn't want to see a way back anyway.

I was also very worried about my son Ray at that stage because I could see that he was starting to drink heavily, too. Even though I was drunk most of the time myself, I could still see him going down the same road as his father and that frightened me. I wasn't any sort of a role model to have, and I had to take some blame for how he was acting, because he saw nothing different at home; it was what he was used to. He had liked his drink before Mena died, but it was more than obvious that he was getting worse and worse as the weeks, months and years went on.

I never needed an excuse to drink, but I had one very bad experience in 2003. Tyrone were playing Down in the Ulster Final of the GAA and the match was being held in Bundoran in County Donegal. Ray and myself headed up to the game in my Nissan Terrano jeep. I had been off the drink and the cigarettes for a few weeks at this stage and was doing OK, but Tyrone were down ten points at half-time and we were all disgusted and the stress was building up and up. For me, this possible defeat was the perfect excuse to go back on the soup and the fags, and that's what I did.

That day we ended up drawing with Down, as Tyrone came back into the game. In fact, we eventually went on to win the All-Ireland. But because I had caved in and started back on the booze, we drank all day and all night and I lost count of how many pints and shorts I got through.

That was how things were back then when there was a big GAA game on. I'd go all out and I'd be on the beer from morning till night, using the excuse that everyone else was doing it anyway, and sure it was a good reason to be out there mixing with people. But it didn't make any difference whether there was a game on or not; it just meant that on days like that everyone else was getting drunk too and I didn't stand out so much in the crowd. It was seen as normal.

What I do remember is waking up at 4:00 a.m. on the sofa, looking around the room and thinking, how the hell did I get back here? I saw the keys of the jeep on the table and I got up and looked out the window and there it was, parked up in the driveway. My stomach turned when I realized that I had driven all the way from Bundoran to Tyrone, a good 40 miles, absolutely drunk. How I got back in one piece without killing someone or wrapping the car around a lamp post, I'll never know. To make matters worse, I don't know how it happened, but I had left Ray in Donegal and I hadn't even realized that I'd done it.

That was the day when I finally accepted that I had to do something about my drinking. I decided that if I was ever going out for a drink again, the keys would be left in the house and I would try my best not to binge, to just try and have a few drinks and leave it at that. I knew that I was very lucky to be alive that night, and lucky that I hadn't killed anyone else on my way home. If I had been stopped by the police, I would have definitely ended up in jail. Then what would have happened to my kids? How would they have felt losing their father as well? It was a strong wake-up call.

I had got to the stage where I basically lived to get to the pub, to get out of the house, but then as soon as I'd get there I'd want to go home. The lads in the pub would be talking about Omagh and stuff and I didn't want to hear it. They meant no harm but I didn't want to be listening to it, because that was what I was trying to escape from in the first place. But I knew that it was going to be a hard job stopping because it was such a part of my daily life. It had become an addiction, and a costly one at that.

I promised myself that I'd give it a shot, but I knew it wouldn't be easy. Every day I was listening to the rumours going around about who was responsible for the blast, the odd things that had happened in the hours prior to the bombing and all the promises by the powers-that-be that it would only be a matter of time before they had those responsible behind bars.

It was so frustrating hearing all these promises and then, bit by bit, realizing that it was all just mouth; that promises given by the governments on both sides in the Republic of Ireland and the UK were all for publicity. All those promises were being made and yet nothing was happening. In the beginning you'd build your hopes up, convinced that it was only a matter of time, but days turned into weeks, weeks into months and then months into years.

We were invited to various meetings in the weeks and months that followed the bomb. Tony Blair, the then British Prime Minister, was over a few days after the attack and he visited the site and met some of the families affected. His wife Cherie spoke to us and I found her to be a very genuine type of person, much more genuine than her husband. In fact, I would go so far as to say that the likes of Tony Blair, Irish Taoiseach Bertie Ahern and other people who had the power to do something to get to the bottom of things, didn't really give a damn about the rest of us. They were only ever concerned about their appearances in the papers and on TV.

We meant nothing to them at the end of the day. They chatted with us, had their pictures taken for the papers and went home to their cosy little beds and slept well. We, on the other hand, were left to live through the hurt and the heartache and no one seemed to give a damn.

Mo Mowlam, who was the Northern Ireland Secretary at the time, was with Blair on his visit and they walked up and down looking at the devastation. Of course, they promised the sun, moon and stars, and Mowlam vowed to catch whoever was responsible, but we waited and waited and nothing happened. For days and weeks after the attack, politicians from both sides of the border and the UK jumped on the bandwagon and swore they would do everything in their power to get those responsible, and of course we wanted to believe them. We didn't have any other hope.

The then President of the United States, Bill Clinton, even visited the site and promised he'd work with the governments to see that those who carried out the bombing faced justice. In fact, we all had a meal in his company and he walked around the tables chatting to people. I didn't say much to him but he spent some time with Shauna and she even got his autograph, which she has to this day.

I spent all my time going to meetings with every Tom, Dick and Harry and we all clung on to the promises they were throwing at us. It was a great publicity stunt for them all, because wherever there were victims of the bombing or families of victims, there were members of the press and photo opportunities for the politicians. But at the end of the day we eventually realized that we were on our own and no one could help us except ourselves.

We went on a trip to Dublin, just weeks after the bombing, on 25 November 1998, just Shauna and myself, to visit the Irish President Mary McAleese. We were looking forward to meeting the President, because she had always come across as a lovely lady on the TV and we had met her on her visit to Omagh a few days after the bombing. Unfortunately, this particular trip was an eye-opener for me.

I made my decision on the bus trip back home to stop attending any ceremonies or any functions in the future to do with Omagh, because I was sickened at the behaviour of a small number of people on the bus. There were three busloads of us in total driving from Omagh to Dublin, up to the Phoenix Park and Áras an Uachtaráin, the President's residence. Shauna and

I thought that it was mostly going to be families of the victims who would be travelling, but it turned out that we were very much in the minority. The buses were filled with people who allegedly were 'helpers' on the day of the bombing.

There were nursing staff from the various hospitals, which was fine, and lads from the leisure centre where we all stayed on the day waiting for news, but then there were fellas who were literally just going up for the day out and were drunk going home. There were even Sinn Féin supporters on the bus on a day when there should have been no politics involved whatsoever.

Shauna and myself were fine on the journey going up, but a nurse asked us to swap buses with her on the way back, as her pals were on our bus. So we got onto the other bus and I was appalled at the carry-on. These louts were absolutely out of their heads on drink, and the bad language and the slagging that took place was a disgrace.

The trip was supposed to be in memory of the people we had lost and yet these fellas took no notice of how we were feeling. All they cared about was how much drink they could get through on the way back. They had bought drink in the North before they got on the buses and it was simply a 'booze cruise' for them. The trip was an absolute joke and I turned to Shauna and said to her, 'That's it now as far as I'm concerned. I'll never take part in any of this stuff again,' because it was a total sham. Shauna agreed with me because she could hear the cursing and the slagging that was going on, and in her mind that day was a day to remember her mother.

On the positive side, meeting Mary McAleese and her husband and family was lovely. We spent a long time talking to the President's husband Martin and they were very friendly and seemed genuinely caring. The Vienna Boys Choir were over from Austria and put on a brilliant performance for us, but the journey home just ruined it all.

There were many occasions when I could have gone to commemorations over the years but I chose not to. But there was one thing that I would have genuinely loved to go to and that was a match organized in Derry on 16 October 1998, just two months after the bombing, when Derry City played a charity game against Mick McCarthy's Ireland squad in the Brandy-well. Niall Quinn, Steve Staunton and even David Ginola came to Derry to take part. Omagh District Council sent me tickets for that match but unfortunately they arrived the day after the game was played. It was a charity game and Ray and myself would have loved to go to meet the likes of Quinn and Ginola.

There was another commemoration in Spain for the victims and survivors from Madrid who were unfortunate enough to be caught up in all the mayhem that day, but unfortunately we didn't get to go; some members of Omagh City Council attended on our behalf. It was bad enough for people from Northern Ireland having to go through what we did, but those poor innocent people from Spain were there simply to enjoy a holiday. They had no connection whatsoever with any sort of politics, yet those who died lost their lives for nothing and those who survived were left with a horrific memory of this country that they will never forget. Just thinking about it all disgusts me.

There was an Omagh Fund set up so the money would go to the families of the victims, but what they didn't tell the people was that there were two sides to the fund, a discretionary end and a charitable end. Some people would have been under the impression when they heard that over £5 million was donated that the families were getting huge handouts and their plight was eased somewhat financially, but that was never the case. Yes, we all received money to help us get over the immediate aftermath of Omagh, but some people were of the belief that we got hundreds of thousands of pounds and that was simply not the case.

About six or seven months after the bombing, when I had started to get my head together a bit, I remember saying that we would never see the day when those responsible for the bombing would be put behind bars. We'd heard all the promises from the politicians north and south of the border, and yet nothing was being done. And I wasn't wrong. But no matter what delays and obstacles were put in the way, I was determined, and still am, to fight until the bitter end to get justice for Mena. If I sat back and just accepted things as they were, I'd be letting her down and there would be no reason for me living.

Maybe that's what kept me going when I eventually recovered the drive to start looking after my family, to hand back my gun and stop selfishly thinking of taking my own life. Mena was always my driving force, pushing me on all the time. It took a long time, many years in fact, for me to realize this.

I have learned in recent times that there is a right time and a right place for everything and you will only ever get something out of counselling when you are truly ready to move on. The year 2004 was my time to do just that. I eventually went back to the counsellor in the Tara Centre in Omagh, and I truly believe that is why I am still alive today. The main reason I went back for help was that I had come to a very big crossroads in my life, a point that I could never have imagined coming to, and my mind was all over the place. I was traumatized by guilt and a huge fear of moving on. It was this stint of counselling that persuaded me to totally change the course of my life and do something I could never have dreamt was possible.

Chapter 4

A Visit from Romania

One Thursday evening in February, 1997, Mena and I were sitting down for a cup of tea in the kitchen when, out of the blue, she started to tell me about a meeting that was coming up in the Royal Arms Hotel in Omagh. She had read an article in the local papers, the *Ulster Herald* and the *Tyrone Constitution*, appealing for families who might be interested in caring for young children who were coming over from orphanages in Romania. Mena told me she wanted to take a child who was coming over from the former communist country for a break during the summer holidays.

The subject had never been mentioned before in our house; we had never talked about Romania and neither of us knew a thing about the place, let alone the language. But Mena was determined to find out as much as she could about how you would go about this process and what you would be required to do to fund the visit.

At first I was totally against it, but Mena was insistent that we both go along to this meeting to hear more and see if it was for us. She probably knew that, once I'd heard some of the horrific stories of how these children lived, I'd change my mind immediately and let her go ahead with her plan. So off we went to the hotel. I was very surprised to see how many people had turned up, considering that very little was really known about Romania at the time and the idea of bringing children over from a foreign country for a holiday was all very new to us in Northern Ireland.

That night I met a woman called Elaine Armstrong, and another organizer from Drumquin who had taken it on himself to try to get these children over. Elaine spoke to the group gathered and told us that they were initially planning to bring just ten girls and boys to Tyrone that year, and they were setting up this group along with the support of the Northwest Romanian Relief Fund, based in Derry. They told us that we would need to raise £400 sterling each if we were serious about taking in one of the children. They explained the importance of the breaks for these kids, who had never experienced a holiday in their short little lives and lived a basic life with few or no toys, no sweets, no trips away and no life outside of the orphanage gates. They were basically existing in the most frugal of accommodation and had none of the accepted luxuries that other 'normal' children in Northern Ireland, or any other Western country for that matter, simply took for granted. We heard how they were living in rundown orphanages where their days were filled only with schoolwork and their nights spent sleeping in cramped dormitories with dozens of others. They had no life other than that inside the walls of these children's refuges.

We were all touched by what was said at the meeting; you'd have to have a heart of stone not to be. It made me realize just how lucky I was and how lucky my own children were. If Mena had planned for me to be shocked that night and agree to go ahead with her plan, then she was right. Having listened to the way of life in this country, so far away from our own little island, I knew that we had to do our bit to give some poor child a holiday that he or she would remember for a long time. So we started to plan how we would raise the cash to get one of these young orphans over to Drumquin.

Mena was raring to go and she pulled out all the stops to make sure that we raised as much money as possible to ensure that we were able to look after one of these poor kids. We ran discos and other functions in the local youth centre over the following weeks, and the reaction was brilliant. Fair play to Mena, she managed to raise more money than anyone else in the group. Because of all her hard work and the amount of money she succeeded in getting that year, she was given first choice of which of the children she wanted to take in for a fortnight in July.

Elaine came to the house one day with a heap of photos and set them down in front of us. It was very hard for us to say which of them we wanted to look after because they were all so beautiful and we knew that they all needed to be cared for. Eventually, Mena picked this gorgeous wee girl with very dark skin and black hair, who was photographed sitting on a sofa and smiling. Her name was Andreea. We were so excited about meeting her.

All of our own children were looking forward to the visit and having someone new in the house who looked totally different to anyone else in the area and spoke a different language. On the day of her arrival it was absolute mayhem as the children waited to see wee Andreea, whom we were told was just nine years old. They had cleaned their rooms for hours and Shauna had her toys left out, ready for her new friend to play with. Andreea was going to sleep in the girls' bedroom with them and everything was in place for her.

We were told that she would be picked up from Dublin Airport with the other kids and Elaine would take her back to her own mother's house in Drumquin, where we were to pick her up. Mena was delighted when we walked through the door and saw little Andreea for the first time. She was absolutely gorgeous and seemed really smiley. We couldn't wait to get her back to the house to meet the rest of the kids. It must all have been very strange for this little one, because where we lived was obviously totally different from where she was living. There was so much for her to take in, with a new family and new sur-roundings. It had been her first time on an aeroplane as well.

By the time we got to our house it was already 10:00 p.m. and Andreea was absolutely shattered, so she briefly met every-one, got her hugs from the girls, and then went straight up to bed. She had a little bag with her which held a toothbrush, a tube of toothpaste, a pair of pyjamas and a roll of toilet paper that would have taken the skin off a horse's backside. It was like the cheap woodchip wallpaper that was in many houses years ago, when no one had any money; it was rough as hell. She had no clothes other than the ones on her back that day.

Even though she was drained when she arrived, Andreea got up a couple of hours later and she was full of life. Within min-utes she was doing cartwheels across the floor with the others. She settled in immediately and the language barrier soon meant nothing. What the others did, she did, and somehow they all understood each other. She had a good sleep that first night and seemed to love her new bedroom, but the next morning when the food was put on the table, she didn't know what to eat. All the children were stuffing their faces with toast and cornflakes and Andreea didn't know what these things floating around in the bowl were. However, despite her curiosity, whatever we put on the table seemed to disappear.

When Mena went up to the bedroom every day, Andreea would already have her bed made, her pyjamas folded neatly at the bottom of the bed and her panties washed and hanging over the sink in the bathroom to dry. That was what she had to do in the orphanage and so she carried on with that routine and we said nothing.

One day Mena lifted Andreea's pillow and discovered that the sheet was covered in toast and crumbs. The poor wee thing had been sneaking the food up to her room every day and hiding it under the pillow in case she'd need it later. That was what she was used to doing in the orphanage because they got so little to eat; she thought it was going to be the same in our house. We also realized that she was using her own toilet paper, the lethal stuff she had brought over with her, until she eventually noticed that our stuff was much softer than hers; once she found this out, she abandoned her roll of sandpaper for the softer option.

Her English wasn't good at all and she found it hard to communicate with us sometimes, so if she was in bad humour she'd make a huffing noise and pull a frown. But Mena wasn't a woman who'd suffer fools gladly and she treated Andreea as if she were one of our own. One morning when Andreea started her usual huffing and puffing over something, Mena gave the kitchen table a massive wallop with her fist and Andreea nearly jumped out of her skin with the fright. She never huffed after that. The truth was, she was getting spoiled and she obviously thought that she could push that little bit more each day, but she hadn't bargained on Mena retaliating.

From that day on she was great; she just rolled in with the rest of them, did what she was told and ate what everyone else was eating. The kids loved her and Shauna was especially close to her, taking over as if she were the big sister, as there were only a couple of years between them. The two of them got on great and Andreea was clearly enjoying herself. During those two weeks we took trips around the North in the car, and on the days she wasn't out for a drive, the kids entertained themselves with all sorts of games.

Andreea learned a lot of English words along the way – some we were glad of and others that we weren't! She listened to everything and she used everything she heard, good and bad. She loved to watch *Aladdin* on video and if she'd had her way she'd have watched it 24 hours a day. It was on so much that it would have driven you up the walls. They wouldn't have had videos in the orphanage, so it was a huge attraction for her.

I have to admit we spoiled her rotten. The amount of presents she got was mad. We hadn't much money at that time but we bought her little dresses and shoes. My mother and the neighbours also bought her clothes and other things, and she had three big bags going back when they were only meant to have one. (I later learned from experience that these children weren't even getting to keep this stuff. As soon as they got back to the orphanage, the clothes were taken off them and distributed to all the other children. We all learned our lesson over time and stopped sending stuff out in bulk. We eventually only shipped donations through the relief fund and through the drivers who were delivering aid. It was the only way to know that your hard-earned money was going exactly where you wanted it to go.)

However, we noticed how Andreea's personality started to change in the days before she was due to go home, and that hurt us. When she knew the day of her return was looming, she got very down. We would catch her sitting on her own, looking very sad. That was hard for us to see, because Mena would have given anything not to have to send her back.

Andreea had such a good time with us and saw a totally different side to life, so we knew it was going to be a huge upheaval to have to go back to her normal daily routine, locked up all day behind the huge walls of an orphanage where she had little or no freedom and absolutely no luxuries. Toys, sweets, going for family drives in the car around the countryside and shopping trips would soon be just a distant memory for her, and we could clearly see that she was getting down thinking about her return.

I remember how upset Andreea was the night she was going back. She was sobbing and hugging everyone and it broke our hearts. She was getting very attached by now to the family and she had everything she could have ever wanted with us. I remember saying to Mena that if we had kept her and not sent her on the bus back to Dublin, she probably wouldn't have been missed anyway. That particular year, about 130 kids came in on the flight from Romania, and that was only on one week and there were only a handful of minders with them, so they'd have had a hard job keeping track of everyone. However, much as we wanted to hold on to her, we knew we couldn't. We had to do everything by the book.

It was very hard for us to let her go. To be honest, I hadn't wanted to take any child over in the first place, but I never thought that I would get so attached to her, and so quickly. Over those two weeks she became just like one of our own and I was worried about her leaving us, because none of us knew what she was actually going back to. We knew nothing about her circumstances and we didn't know what had happened to her family or how she had come to live in an orphanage. All of those things hung over us like a big black cloud as we handed her back to the organizers and they headed on their journey back up to Dublin to catch the flight home.

When we agreed to take a child from Romania, we got no information about their background, their families, their living circumstances or their education. We knew nothing at all about their lives in Romania –what sort of food they ate, what sort of clothes they wore or anything else. Back then we had little access to computers and, even if we had, we wouldn't even have known where to start finding out about Romanian life and culture. So we asked no questions and we got no answers. Knowing nothing made us all even more worried for Andreea's future. She was a beautiful young thing and when she left we didn't know if we would ever see her again.

The house had been manic for those two weeks in July, because every child in the area called to play with 'the new girl'. There were 30 houses in McCrea Park and the children from every house on the road were up at ours every day. Andreea was a huge novelty for everyone and she got on with them all, despite the language barrier. It's very funny how children adapt to any circumstances put in front of them and how they can communicate without words with simple little things like dolls and teddy bears. They are amazing little people who let nothing create a barrier when it comes to playing. They just get on with it.

I know it broke Mena's heart to have to say goodbye to little Andreea, not knowing what lay ahead for her in her home country. Mena was so upset that she said she couldn't commit to taking her back again, because it broke her heart to see her go. However, though I had been the sceptical one at the beginning, I swore that, no matter what, that little child was coming back to us the next summer. I went to the lads in the relief organization in Derry, Sean Boyle and Michael Newton, and I told them that if they were bringing the kids back the following summer, we wanted Andreea. I'd do whatever it took to make sure that happened. And I did. In fact, I still have the marks on my backside to prove it, as I rode 300 miles on a bicycle to raise the money to bring them back.

As the arrangements were being made for the next group of orphans to come over the following year, I rallied the troops. I was still in touch with all my pals from the Nestlé factory at the time and we had done three bike rides in 1995, 1996 and 1997 for various charities in the area, so the lads decided that 1998 would be the year for Romania.

A group of us cycled from Omagh to Longford on the Monday, got absolutely hammered in the Longford Arms that night, and got on the bike again the next day and rode over the beautiful Curlew Mountains into Sligo. It was a tough cycle, driving along some very badly potholed roads, but the scenery was amazing and the craic was great. We stayed overnight in a hotel in the town, where we had our fill of beer. The next day we headed back to Omagh through the holiday resort of

Bundoran in County Donegal, a lot worse for wear, with sore bottoms and sore heads. We were lucky that the weather wasn't bad and that we had no casualties along the way. It all went along nice and smoothly.

That year we raised £6,000 sterling for the fund and we were delighted. We held a dance in a marquee at the back of the O'Ceathain Arms when we got home, to present the cyclists with a trophy for all the hard work they'd put in to raise the money. No one could have imagined we'd have achieved such a huge amount for a first cycle in aid of a country so far away.

Brendan Shine, who is a very well-known singer in Ireland, played for us that night. Everyone had to have at least £100 sponsorship to even get up on a bike for that trip, and the support we got was amazing. I had a lot of business contacts and they all put their hands into their pockets without a second thought when I approached them.

When those children arrived for their second trip, we all knew why we did it and the sores on my backside were worth it. I remember thinking at the time that if I never did anything again in my life for anyone, I could be happy knowing that I did what I could to give a child who had nothing some kind of a break in life. Just to see the looks of joy on those children's faces when they were with their holiday families would bring a tear to anyone's eye. Those weeks were the highlight of the year for us all.

Thank God, Andreea came back to us. This time she would be with us for three weeks. We had waited a full year for her to come back, and for that whole year we talked about her non-stop, wondering what she was up to in Romania. Was she safe? Did she have enough food? We knew nothing about the situation in Romania, only what we would have witnessed on TV documentaries at the time about the orphanages in Eastern Europe, so it was only natural to worry.

We couldn't wait to see Andreea again. We organized a bus to pick the kids up on the second visit, as once again they were arriving into Dublin Airport. A man called Charlie Lynch drove his bus there and back free of charge for us, and Shauna and myself headed up to Dublin, dying to see Andreea again.

I remember that particular visit so well, because we waited and waited at the airport and there was no sign of her. All of the other kids were out and all excited about their holiday. Until Andreea walked through those doors, we wouldn't have known whether she was on that flight or not. There was no way of checking. So that particular night, our hearts were in our mouths as we walked up and down the arrivals hall in Dublin Airport, praying that she had got on the flight.

When she eventually emerged with her little rucksack, she ran straight over to the two of us. She was thrilled to be back. She had been learning to speak English in school over in the orphanage and, this time round, her grasp of the language was much better and she was able to talk to our children in broken English. It was great both for her and the rest of us. From the time she had gone back the year before until she arrived back in 1998, we were planning her next trip. I had wanted to take her over for Christmas on that first year but I was told that there were no trips at that time of year. (I found out later that was not the case at all). But these visits were a learning process.

The second holiday was fantastic. We all went off as a family to John Murphy's caravan park in Ballina in County Mayo, right beside the beach. The weather wasn't great, even though it was August, but it was a break. When it rained we were all stuck in the caravan with the raindrops pelting off the roof, but in fairness to the kids they said nothing, played games and kept themselves occupied. When the sun came out, it was straight down to the beach to swim and build sandcastles. Andreea loved it; it was an experience she had never had before and it was fantastic to see a huge smile on her face all the time. The beach was something our own children were well used to and thought nothing of, but for Andreea it was like a scene from a fairy tale.

However, once again we knew the dream was going to come to an end and she had to go back to her life in Romania. We saw the change in Andreea again in the days coming up to D-Day. We could see the pain in her eyes, knowing that she had to leave this little fantasy land. We didn't have much money; we were simple working-class people with a small average house. Like most people, we had the worry of where the money was coming from for the next lot of bills. But to Andreea, we had a huge house, loads of money and a great life.

It was just so different to what she was seeing in her home country – the poverty, the starving disabled children begging on the streets and the lack of the most basic of facilities. She spent her time inside the walls of a dilapidated building with other kids in the same position as herself and she had no real life, not what we would call a normal life for a child.

I began to wonder back then if we were actually doing the right thing by taking her out of what was her own comfort zone and showing her what she could have if she'd had the good fortune to have been born in another country, to another family. I wondered if it was damaging to these kids to put them through all of this and then send them back to such a horrible life.

One night when we had a charity bash for the children in the O'Ceathain Arms I met up with a woman called Doina, who cared for Andreea and some of the other kids in the orphanage in Fagaras, and I asked her out straight if we were actually damaging these youngsters by bringing them over in the first place. Her answer made me realize once and for all that what we were doing was in fact a godsend to these young kids. She said that those trips enabled the children to see that there was another life outside of Romania and outside of the orphanages, and it made them think that when they grew up they would aspire to having a similar life for themselves and their own families. They had something to focus on for their future. That comforted me a bit.

But it was still hard to let go. On 9 August – the Sunday before the bomb – Mena said her goodbyes and she was too upset to hang around. She wouldn't even come to the airport with us.

A day or two later, Mena and I were talking about the previous few days and how much we had all enjoyed the time we'd had with Andreea. I had promised Andreea that I would do my best to get out to Romania and visit her before her next trip back. We were chatting about this and planning how we might be able to do it, as the flights were quite pricey at the time. I asked Mena what she thought about the possibility of adopting Andreea and she said that it would be a huge responsibility, but something that she would think seriously about, because she was becoming very attached to her.

So that was our plan. We hadn't a clue how we were going to go about it but we would at least find out what it involved and how much it would cost. Once we knew all that, we could make our decision.

But it was never to be. Just six days later, Mena was murdered and our lives were destroyed. My plan to go into the travel agents that day to price the flights never happened, and my priority for the immediate future was to look after Shauna and the kids. I never imagined that I would fall apart as well.

However, as time went on our thoughts turned back to Andreea. We knew she would be devastated to hear that Mena had been murdered. She wouldn't have understood 'why', or that our country was at war. She would have known nothing about the Troubles and the years of violent history that people on the north side of the border had had to endure. Dying suddenly would be one thing, but being deliberately blown up by a bomb on a busy street as you shopped with your family was something most people would only see in a film or on TV. We wondered if we would ever see Andreea again; and if we did, would she ever feel the same about us? Would she want to come back to Tyrone again, now that Mena was gone? All of these things were a concern.

We talked as a family about what Mena would have wanted and we decided that, no matter what happened in the future, she would have wanted us to go to Romania, despite the cost, and fight for Andreea. We realized that it would be costly to travel back and forth, pay for visas, etc. I wasn't working and we didn't have much savings, but we made the decision that even if it meant me borrowing money, then this was what I would do. As far as we were concerned, Mena's wish would have been to do all we could to give that child a better life, especially now that we had lost the one person who had kept the whole family together. Besides, the distraction of having Andreea around would help to keep the kids focused and give them something to work at. If we were successful in her adoption, then we knew that Mena would have been happy. So Shauna and myself set about planning the trip.

In October of 1999 I finally made my first trip out to Romania, with Shauna. I was going with one thing in mind, and one thing only: to start the adoption process for Andreea. It was to be a bittersweet trip, but we went over with a group of lads and the craic was great. They really helped to lift our spirits.

Word had got out about our plan to adopt this little girl, as the papers had taken a big interest in the kids from their first visit to the area. It was plastered all over the papers at the time that I was going to adopt a little Romanian girl and the *Belfast Telegraph*, the *Irish News* and some other local paper said they would help with financing the adoption in whatever way they could. The media took a huge interest in it and most papers, on either side of the border, had something about our trip to Fagaras to take Andreea back home.

Elaine Armstrong came with us on this trip, as did her mother, Linda Fyffe, and I brought Shauna. Elaine was one of the women who had organized the initial trips to Drumquin two years before, in 1997, and she was looking forward to seeing the way things operated herself so that she'd have a better idea of what life was like out there when she was looking for people to take children in for the holidays. We were all really excited about seeing the place, and of course Shauna and myself were looking forward to seeing Andreea, but dreading having to break the news to her about Mena's death.

We were due to arrive in Bucharest at 4:00 p.m. on Sunday,

and the lads in Derry were to have organized a minibus to pick us up, but the man who was to make the arrangements went on holiday and forgot about us altogether. So we arrived at the airport and waited and waited. We ended up going to the train station in a beaten-up taxi, where we sat until 9:00 p.m., waiting on a train that would take us to Fagaras. We can look back and laugh at it now, but the taxi driver we got that night was a greedy article and would have robbed the tooth out of your head. He was trying to rip us off whatever way he could, and had we not been advised that this would happen before we arrived, we would have been stung big time. We paid him what we knew the fare should be and a little bit over the odds. I could see he was totally angry that his plan hadn't worked. Most people wouldn't have a clue when they arrived how much it should cost to get from one place to another, so he must have had a nice little scam going for any foreigners visiting the area. At that time you would get about three or four packets of cigarettes for £1 sterling, or a big glass of vodka for 25p. So these guys knew that picking up an English or Irish tourist who didn't know the lie of the land could net them a huge sum of money by Romanian standards, and keep them going for a few weeks, never mind days.

Money is so hard to come by in Romania that at the train station we literally had to sit on the suitcases for the whole time, because there were hoards of youngsters running around us begging us to let them carry our cases for a few bob. If we hadn't sat on them, there was no two ways about it but they would have vanished in a split second. These kids were desperate and the sight of a stranger filled them with excitement at the prospect of what they might be able to either beg for or steal.

They'd have robbed the eyes out of your head if they thought they'd get away with it.

Our train journey prepared us for what conditions might be like all over Romania. When we went to use the toilet, we discovered that whatever you deposited there went straight out onto the tracks. There was no toilet bowl, cistern or anything like that; it was simply a hole in the floor with feet marks that kept your feet from slipping. If you hadn't bought the 'sand-paper' at the train station, then you'd have to walk around with a dirty arse until you reached your destination, because toilet roll was not a luxury that existed on the transport system in Romania. If someone had told us this, we wouldn't have believed them.

There was an armed soldier at each end of the carriage, taking in everyone and everything on that train and ready, and I'd say well able, to shoot at will. They were armed to the teeth and they were only young lads. They helped us off with our luggage at Fagaras and they were very friendly youngsters, but I could see the hardship on everyone's faces, from soldiers to passengers. It was obvious from the moment we arrived in Romania that no amount of horror stories we had heard could have prepared us for what we were about to witness for ourselves.

We eventually got into Fagaras at 2:30 a.m., where we were to meet up with the minibus that would take us to the hotel, which was right opposite the orphanage. It had been pre-booked for us so that we would be right beside the orphanage all the time. It was to cost us the equivalent of a pound a night, and we quickly saw why. Jesus, it was rough. But we were so tired at that stage that we all just fell asleep. I was gobsmacked when I woke up the next morning because, although it had looked bad in the dark when we were all drained with tiredness, it was a complete hell-hole in the light of day. Poor Shauna nearly died when she woke up and looked around her.

There was a bit of carpet on the stairs about 18 inches wide and it didn't cover the whole step, so as you walked up the stairs, it walked down. It wasn't stapled in at all and every morning the woman who ran the place took it up, shook it out and placed it down again. She probably prayed that someone didn't break their necks on it in the meantime.

The bedroom consisted of a bed and nothing else. What looked like a wardrobe turned out to be a big stove, which was where the heating came from. None of the bedrooms had a bathroom or even a toilet. I got up in the middle of the night to use the loo and found it was a hole in the ground. When I opened the door I was nearly washed down the stairs with the urine on the floor. The smell was sickening and I had to stand on all this urine to go to the toilet myself and try to block out the stink that was wafting around the room.

The bath was covered in green moss and there was a lump of pipe sticking out of the ceiling – that was the shower – and the room itself was filthy. I didn't have a bath for a week until I came home. I could actually smell myself coming home on the plane, but it was better than risking catching some bloody illness standing in that filthy room with dirty water dripping from the pipe in the roof.

God forbid you asked for food, because you just didn't get any. We were told that there was no point in moving to another hotel because they were all the same. There were no four-star hotels, or even two-star ones for that matter, in Fagaras. So we just had to make do with what we had and be grateful. We dreaded going back to it in the evening time but we didn't have much of a choice. We can look back now and laugh, but at the time it didn't seem funny at all.

On our first morning in Fagaras we were woken at 7:15 a.m. by Lenuta, a wee girl from the orphanage, who knew that I was coming over to see Andreea. She banged down the door because we were in a deep sleep, absolutely shattered from the manic trip over. She announced that Andreea's mammy was waiting for me at the orphanage.

I was in shock and I kept asking, how could Andreea's mother be there if she was an orphan? But I was told that this woman was waiting for me because she had heard that I was coming to take her daughter away. I just couldn't believe what I was hearing and I genuinely thought that there was some sort of mistake. I threw my clothes on and headed across the road.

As I walked in through the gate, I could see a small woman standing beside the hut wearing a grey coat. She had a young woman with her who spoke perfect English and whose dialect was so good that you'd have sworn she'd come from Ardboe. As the woman spoke, the interpreter translated it into English. She basically said that she'd been there all night because she had heard that I had come to take her daughter. She had been sitting at that hut in the freezing cold all night in case I came and she missed me.

I felt so sorry for her, because God only knows how she was thinking. She didn't know what I was or who I was. To her I was simply a strange man who was coming to Romania to take away her child. She wasn't to know that I was of the opinion that Andreea had no mother or father and that I was simply there to give her a new and better chance at life in a country where she could have had many more opportunities and a loving family. Through the interpreter I explained that I knew nothing about her existence.

Despite a tense stand-off initially, she began to relax and understand that I was the one there who had been misled and that I wasn't there to kidnap her little girl.

I didn't blame Andreea for not telling me that she had a mother, because in fairness to her the subject had never come up before. Even if she had wanted to tell us, she might not have had the words to do it. When you hear that a child lives in an orphanage you automatically presume that she is an orphan, that she is there because she has no family to care for her. But that wasn't the case at all. I later found out that a lot of the children in these places had in fact got parents but they were in care because their families could not afford to look after them with food and clothes and provide an education. And it turned out that Andreea was no different.

I found out that day that she had a sister called Nicoletta who was also in care, but whom I hadn't heard about before. Nicoletta was older than Andreea. I heard that plans were already in place to send Nicoletta to a family in the north of Ireland for Christmas. This was the first time that I had been aware of the fact that it was even possible to take these kids over for the Christmas break, so I asked Andreea's mother, who it turned out was called Maria, if she would allow me to bring Andreea over to us that year. This was in October and I knew time wasn't on my side if I was to get everything sorted for the Christmas break. She agreed, because she knew that Andreea was in safe hands with us and that she had enjoyed her other trips over to our home. She finally realized that I wouldn't try to kidnap her child and that it had all been just a big misunderstanding on everyone's part.

We were obviously upset that things had gone totally askew for us. We had come over with the intention of setting the wheels in motion to adopt Andreea, and now we didn't know where we stood. Of course we were happy for Andreea that she had a mother and that she hadn't been left an orphan in some horrible circumstances, but we were also very disheartened.

When we got to meet Andreea, we just told her that Mena had gone to heaven; we didn't go into details of what had happened, as she was only a child and she probably wouldn't have understood anyway. She was clearly upset but we didn't dwell on it at all, we just went on as normal. We didn't want to upset her and then leave her behind on her own thinking about it.

In the days that followed, we got to know Maria a bit more. She had known about Mena through Andreea and she tried to express her feelings to us. We knew by her facial expressions what she was trying to say, and we appreciated her thoughtfulness.

She invited us up to her flat, which was absolutely tiny. There was one room which was made into a bedroom at night by pulling down the settee into a double bed. You couldn't have swung a cat in the kitchen, and the toilet was the same. As you sat on the toilet, you could have had a shower at the same time, because the shower pipe was attached to the cistern and you just pulled a string to get the hot water running. However, everything was well kept and neat and tidy, and I felt so guilty because she went all out to look after us on our visits by making food and buying drinks.

I knew that the few biscuits and the little spread she put on that day must have cost her a fair few bob, and I knew that it was money she couldn't afford. But she was delighted to be able to provide us with a bite to eat. For that is the way of life there.

I didn't have much at home – we didn't have outrageous luxuries – but what we did have I felt very grateful for, having witnessed the level of poverty and yet the level of respect given to foreigners by these people who scrimped and saved just to put food on the table for their families every day. There was very little I could do to change their way of life and I realized that, although they had nothing of value in terms of material goods, they loved their country and they loved their lifestyle, albeit difficult at times.

We knew that Maria was probably spending everything she had on us that week so that she wasn't embarrassed about how little she actually had. She explained that the children came home to her in the little flat every weekend, but having them in the orphanage from Monday to Friday ensured that they were fed and clothed and had an education, things she couldn't have afforded to give them herself.

She was in a relationship at the time with a man, but the children's father, Cozac, was gone. They had split up some time before. She wasn't very long with her new partner but we met him on that first trip, and although it was difficult at times to understand him, we managed somehow to converse. There were always a few people there when we called and there always seemed to be someone who could speak a bit of English, so it wasn't too hard for us to get by.

When we were leaving that first week, Maria signed the papers giving me permission to take Andreea for Christmas. I gave her a bit of money to keep her going and told her not to tell anyone about what I had given her. She was nearly in tears accepting it. It wasn't much, but I knew that it would help her out a bit.

I left her little flat on the last night of our visit and my stomach was sick, because I knew in my heart that something had happened to me that was totally out of my control and I was in an awful situation. I knew the minute I had set eyes on that dark-haired woman shivering in her tightly wrapped grey coat, that there was something about her that had flipped my heart, and that had never happened to me before. Never in my life, since I had met Mena, had I felt anything for another woman. But I knew that I had butterflies in my stomach from the day I first set eyes on her. I felt like a teenager falling in love all over again. Whether I liked it or not, I had fallen for a complete stranger in a strange country and there was nothing I could do about it.

I was riddled with guilt about how I felt and I was ashamed of myself for having any feelings at all for this person whom I didn't even know. In my head I had no right to even look at another woman, never mind feeling attracted to her. It was a situation that was to cause me heartache and concern for a very long time, but for now I had to get on with my life and do whatever was best for little Andreea and my own family back in Northern Ireland. My feelings, whatever they were, had to be put on the back-burner.

I had to try to forget this little Romanian woman whose big brown eyes told her harsh life story without even speaking a single word. They say the eyes are the windows to the soul, and every time I looked into hers I felt the pain of what she was going through, and what she had already gone through in her short life. She was just 33 when we first met. I knew it was killing her to have to hand her children over to the care of the State and that if she could change her life she would, in the blink of an eye. I knew that I may have been her only saving grace. I had little enough money myself, but I had the ability to raise money through fundraising events to try to change the lives of at least a handful of the Romanian people I had met in Fagaras. I knew that God had sent me there for some reason. It was becoming fairly obvious very quickly that the very reason could have been to make me realize what others were going through hundreds of miles away from my home, and that no matter how bad a situation I was in, there was always someone else in a worse state somewhere in the world.

I was without my wife, but if it hadn't been for Mena I wouldn't have been in Romania in the first place. I had never had any interest in visiting the country; I hadn't been keen on taking a child from that country into our home in the first place. Yet the woman who had organized it all was gone and I was now left to pick up the pieces, and I felt I was meant to visit Fagaras. That day in Omagh I never had the chance to price the flights as planned, yet here I was standing in this strange country with Shauna, knowing that we were meant to come. It was fate. And you cannot change fate.

So I promised myself that I would do whatever was in my power to try to help these children, these orphanages, who were struggling to get through each day, and to help this poor woman whose one wish in life was to be a provider for her family.

Chapter 5

Fundraising for the Orphanages

On the flight back home after that first trip, I made a promise to myself to start fundraising immediately. When I got home I started spreading the word about life in Romania and the hardships I had witnessed first-hand. People were genuinely interested, genuinely concerned. In fact, the people in our area were fantastic. Every time I asked for something, I got it. No matter how hard times were for some families, they still managed to dig into their pockets and pull out a few bob for us for whatever cause it may have been, whether it was for bringing a child over on holiday or for sending over to the orphanages.

I kept in contact with Maria and with the orphanage. As needs arose I made it my business to try to get whatever it was that was needed, and I would send it off either by post or with the lads who were driving over in convoy.

In 1999 I ran a big night in our own area, in the O'Ceathain Arms pub. We had a singer called Declan Nerney playing for us, and we charged everyone £10 to get in. I'd been in the audience of *The Late Late Show* on RTÉ just before the gig and I'd been given a weekend for two in the Jury's Hotel in Dublin as part of the audience giveaway, so I put it up as a prize for the raffle that night, along with other vouchers, boxes of chocolates and the usual spot-prize stuff. We charged everyone £5 for a ticket for the draw. That night turned out to be a huge success, more than we could have ever wished for, and we got massive support from the locals. By the time we got all the money in, we realized that we'd made a clear profit of about £8,000. That money was used to bring a group of children over for a holiday to Northern Ireland and it was a huge help. Patrick O'Kane, the owner of the pub, actually paid for the marquee and any other expenses himself, and once he had counted out whatever profit he had made on the bar, he handed over half of that cash to me as well. That is something I will take to my grave in appreciation.

There was a group of us working together to get the money in – myself, Patrick O'Kane, Brian and Seamus Lunney, Elaine Armstrong, Linda Fyffe, Raymond Acheson, Maeve Sheridan and Aidan McCrossan. We all worked together and we raised a huge sum of money by organizing a collection around the families in the area and a follow-up night in the local GAA club to help towards the building of a new orphanage in Fagaras. We knew it would take some time to build this new facility but we were determined to help as much as we could.

We held many a night in the local parish hall, with great singers like Jimmy Buckley and Mick Flavin performing. Another night, when we were due to have a very well-known singer called Johnny Loughrey, we got a call from him to say that he was very sick and wasn't able to appear, but that he was sending along a singer called Farmer Dan in his place. It was a great success. Johnny called me one day, months later, to say he wanted to make it up to me, that he felt really bad about not being able to have made the gig.

As he promised, he performed for another fundraiser in the hall, and it was a brilliant night. Unfortunately, just four months later Johnny died from cancer. I will never forget his generosity despite his illness and everything else that was going on in his life at the time. People like Johnny will always be remembered.

But back in 1999, I made plans with a man called Roger Rene from Belfast, who brought Romanian children to Northern Ireland each Christmas, to bring Andreea over to us that Christmas. The whole family were dying to see her. Up until then her visits always took place in the summer months, but we knew that Christmas would be a much better time to bring her over and treat her a bit. We had planned to have the house covered in Christmas decorations and do everything we could to make sure it would be a holiday she would never forget.

A couple of weeks after I got home from my first trip, I rang the orphanage to see how things were with Andreea. I'd normally ring every Wednesday, but no matter when I'd call I never managed to get to speak to her. Each time I was told that she wasn't around, or they didn't know where she was. Then one day, after a number of calls getting nowhere, I eventually got to speak to Doina, who was in charge, and she told me that the girls were at home with their mother. She told me that when I went home to Northern Ireland, Maria had taken both the children from the home and she was now taking care of them full-time herself.

It seemed the money I had given her before I left in October meant that she no longer had to scrimp and save to put food on the table and have heat in the little flat. It enabled her to bring them back home for good. Seemingly Maria had started to save a few bob from the time Mena was alive, when

Mena had given Andreea a few pounds before she headed back to Fagaras. Andreea would put the money in her sock so that no one robbed it from her, and then when she'd meet her mother she'd hand it straight over to her. Maria had been saving this money in the hope that one day she'd have enough put away to take her kids back. The money I'd handed over before I left was the little extra she'd needed to make that possible. I was absolutely delighted when I heard what had happened and it made everything worthwhile for me.

However, within days of me ringing the orphanage I received a letter from Fagaras apparently signed by Maria and written in broken English. The letter asked me for more money and directed me as to how I should send it over through Western Union. I totally ignored it, thinking that if she was trying to rip me off, I was not going to reply. If she wanted it badly enough, she'd ring me. But I never got that call. I was not only annoyed but also upset that she could do that to me. I felt that it was just too cheeky, as I wanted to help as much as I could but I didn't want to be taken for a fool at the same time.

I found out a while later that Maria had never sent the letter at all. She had obviously been telling people how good we were to her and someone jumped on the bandwagon and decided to try their luck by sending a begging letter, forging Maria's signature. I was so glad that I hadn't fallen for it. But in the back of my head I knew that Maria wasn't the type to take people for granted and I was glad that I hadn't called her to ask what the hell was going on.

Andreea came home that Christmas in 1999 and she had a ball. Her older sister Nicoletta came with her, staying with a woman called Nan Bratten in Lack, near Ederney. It was

Nicoletta's first time out of Romania and she loved Ireland. They both had the best Christmas of their young lives. Andreea's face on Christmas Day when she woke in our house to find that Santa had come during the night was priceless. It was as if she had won the lottery and she was over the moon with her presents.

When Andreea went back after that trip it wasn't as hard for us because we all knew that she was with her family and she was a much happier child. Also, she knew that she'd be coming back to us; there was no worrying on either part about that, because she had become part of the family by then and she knew that we would find the money somehow to get her back.

After that particular Christmas I found myself being drawn to Romania more and more. But I was getting very annoyed with the fact that I seemed to be working my chops off trying to get funding to bring children over on holidays to stay with other families and others were simply sitting back and expecting others to raise all the cash needed. There was just a handful of us doing all the work and it became very disheartening, so I decided that I would somehow get the money together myself to bring the two kids over to stay with us. I didn't know how I was going to manage it, but I had faith that one way or another it would fall into place.

One day I was in Dublin for the trial of one of the men suspected of being involved in the Omagh bombing. A group of us headed off to a pub beside the court for a bit of lunch and a pint or two. A man sat down beside me and we started to talk. He knew we were all up for the trial and he asked if one of us was involved in bringing children over from Romania. I told him I was his man and he started talking to me, asking if there was anything I needed. He introduced himself as Henry Robinson and I told him that it cost roughly £500 to bring one child over for a week, so if he was interested in sponsoring, £500 would cover all the costs of getting Andreea over for a week.

He said that wouldn't be a problem at all. Of course I didn't believe him for a minute; here we were in a strange pub in a strange city and this strange man was offering to sponsor a visit, out of the blue. But he insisted that he was sincere and promised that I'd receive the money. He took my name, address and phone number and we went our separate ways.

I thought that was the end of it until the day of Mena's anniversary that year, when an envelope arrived through the door from himself and another man called Charlie Kelly, who to this day I have never met, for £1,000 to bring the two kids over for Christmas. The two men were living in London and yet Henry kept his word, even got another man in with him, to make sure that those two children came back to Ireland the following Christmas.

I was gobsmacked by the generosity of these two men who didn't know me from Adam. What they don't realize is that if it hadn't been for their donation that year, I would have found it very difficult financially to go back out to Romania and to take those children back home. They gave me the funds I needed that time to kickstart things, and they have no idea what that meant to me and how bringing those two children over together to our home changed all of our lives. There were quite a few cases like that – situations where people who either didn't know me or hadn't seen me for many a year offered and gave whatever they could spare to help out. The fact that it arrived on Mena's anniversary made it even more special.

Another example of this sort of scenario was when I was invited to the local council office to meet Prince Charles, back in late 1998. In fact, I was one of the few people in the area who got to meet him and talk to him face to face. My name was just picked out and I went along. We didn't mention the bombing at all. The man had his own troubles too, as it was just a year after the death of Princess Diana, so I wasn't going to bother the man with my own problems that day. When I was introduced to the prince, I started talking about football. Some of the lads had told him that I was a referee and so we started talking about Celtic and Rangers. I found him to be a very nice man, very friendly. It was a very informal chat and I didn't find it the right time or place to talk about the bombing.

However, on that day a man came over to me and put his hands out to shake mine, asking me if I recognized him. I hadn't a clue who this guy was, but he told me that we had gone to school together. His name was Christopher McGale from John Street and his family used to own a bar there. My head was like a sieve and I couldn't place him at all. But he asked me if I was still involved in bringing children over from Romania, as he wanted to give a donation. I went on to tell him what we were up to and how much it cost us to fly a child across. He said he would send me £500. I went away thinking to myself again that that was probably just another person looking to make conversation. I thought no more about it until seven days later, when a cheque arrived through my hall door for £500.

Christopher still owns a share in the family-run Terrace Bar, and over the years, when things were really tight, I'd pick up the phone and ring him. There and then, he'd send over £500 or £1,000 for the charity. He has been a lifesaver.

It's been said to me before that these businesspeople, who sign cheques and send them off to charities, can make their money back by claiming tax exemptions as it's a charity, but these people genuinely cared about what we were doing and I will always be grateful to anyone who helped us get those kids over. If they claimed tax back on their donations, then so be it, but their money went a long way to giving a small number of people a better chance in life.

Another man called John, a businessman who ran a furniture company in Omagh, was absolutely fantastic to me over the years and, although he always wanted to remain anonymous, I want him to know that I will always be grateful for all the help he has given me over the years to get the girls over. All it would take for him to help was a phone call. It's a very rare thing anywhere in the world to have people at the end of a phone ready to help in whatever way they can. This man John played a huge part in helping me to change things in Romania. One major thing he did was to sponsor a wheelchair for a little boy whom he had never met before.

In August 2007, when Nicoletta was getting married in Fagaras, I went over for the wedding. Three days before I was due to go home, they brought me to the house of a friend of Nicoletta's husband in a wee village a few miles away from Fagaras itself. This man had a son who was about 16 years of age, who had been born with severe disabilities. He could do nothing for himself at all and his days were spent lying in bed, totally incapacitated, dependent on his family 24 hours a day, yet he seemed to have a smile for everyone who walked through the front door. Seeing this child lying there would have broken your heart. To sit there and watch this man nursing his child with no hope whatsoever was heartbreaking.

This boy had never been outside his little village because they had no transport, no adapted wheelchair and therefore no way of him seeing the outside world, the sun splitting the trees, the birds flying about and the clouds blowing by in the clear blue sky. I promised his father before I left that I would do everything I possibly could to get his son a wheelchair that would suit his needs, so that they could both have some lease of life. He had been given a wheelchair before some years earlier, but because he was so badly disabled it was of no use to him. He couldn't stabilize himself or sit up straight, and eventually he would slip from the chair onto the ground. So when I came back home I went down to the Red Cross in Omagh. Both the lads running the office there were my former bosses in the Nestlé factory.

I told them what I needed but that I had no way of paying for it and I needed their help. They told me that they had the very thing; it had been donated to them by an American man. It had everything we needed. It lay back so that he could comfortably fall asleep in it and it sat up straight with support so that he couldn't slip out. The lads understood the situation and said they would be happy with whatever donation I could get for the Red Cross. So I rang my old friend John, who immediately wrote out a cheque, no questions asked. It took nearly a whole year to get that chair transported out, because of the logistics needed to carry it, but it was all worthwhile.

The men who delivered it told me that when they arrived at the house and they put this young boy into his new chair and wheeled him out into the fresh air, it made the whole trip across Europe worthwhile. When his father asked him if he wanted to go back inside, the boy just kept nodding his head from side to side letting him know that he was happy to be left there, breathing in the country air and looking up at the sun. That chair changed that child's life forever, and they said that to see the look of happiness on his face said it all.

I haven't been back to Romania since 2007, but when I do get there the first thing I want to do is to visit that young lad to see for myself the change that chair has made to his life. It would have been very easy for that family to have just bundled their child up and put him into an institution, like many have before, but instead they chose to do all they could as parents to care for their son in a situation of dire poverty, with no help whatsoever, and it has to be commended. Many people in Ireland would never have been able to cope with their plight, even with all the mod cons available here, but their courage and conviction shows the true love they have and the respect they have for their child who, through no fault of his own, came into this world with a chronic disability. If I meet another child in Romania in a similar situation in the coming years, I hope to be able to offer him or her the same quality of life that the wheelchair gave to that young boy.

The hardships some of these children have to endure are heartbreaking. There was one child, a twin called Josef, who was due to come to a family in Drumquin one Christmas but never arrived. When I went out to Romania on the following trip, I made it my business to find out what had happened to him. The flight had been paid for and the family had waited and waited at the airport in Dublin for him to come out. They were devastated when he failed to turn up. Everything had been put in place for his visit and there was no explanation given by anyone for why he had failed to get there. So, when I got to

Romania, I went on a hunt to find him. From what we knew his twin, a little girl, was living with another boy; she was 14 years old and this would have been perfectly legal over there.

I was determined to get to the bottom of what had happened to Josef and let the host family know what the circumstances were. The last I had heard was that he was staying in the orphanage in Codlea, but he wasn't there when we arrived and so we were taken to an orphanage in Brasov, but he wasn't there either. But until the day I die, I will never forget the scene that confronted us at Brasov: there were wee tots standing up in old battered cots, begging us to take them up, with their arms stretched up into the air and tears in their eyes, sobbing. It was the most heartbreaking thing I have ever seen.

There was one little 18-month-old beauty called Roxanna. She was standing on a mattress in a creaky cot which was covered in blue mould and she had a big smile on her face and was beckoning me to take her up. She was covered from head to toe in faeces and the smell was atrocious. I would have loved nothing better than to take that child up out of the disgusting surroundings she had been forced to live in and bring her home with me. It broke my heart to have to turn away from this little tot and walk off. Yet this was not an unusual situation; there were hundreds more just like little Roxanna, abandoned in orphanages all over Romania with no one to love or care for them. But we had no choice but to leave her behind.

The five of us – Shauna, Seamus Lunney, Aidan McCrossan, Raymond Acheson and myself – carried on with our search for Josef, still in shock at what we had just witnessed. A child on the street eventually showed us where this little boy lived. We gave her a few bob and she ran off, delighted with herself.

The place she directed us to looked desolate. There were cows living in better conditions than some of these people, and the place had an awful depressive feeling about it. We saw this little boy standing at the end of the road with no shirt on him, no toes in his shoes and clearly living in abject poverty. The father came out to us and the interpreter explained who we were and why we were there. After some time talking, the father finally allowed us to take Josef off to a restaurant not too far away for something to eat. He literally gave the boy the shirt off his own back to wear for the trip.

The boy was filthy dirty and was delighted to be going off to a fast food place for a burger and chips. His expression was priceless as he gobbled up his food. We knew that he had probably never been to a fast food restaurant in his life and probably never expected to go into one. When we dropped him back home, the father promised that he would let him go on the next trip to Ireland.

However, the same thing happened again and Josef never arrived. We were all very concerned at this stage for his safety and so, on the next trip at Easter, we headed off to where he lived again to see what had happened and if he was all right. There, once again, we met the same wee girl on the street and she recognized us immediately. She told us that this little lad had moved from the house and she eagerly brought us up to the house where he was now staying.

It turned out that he had moved in with his aunt and uncle and there were eight of them living, eating and sleeping in the one tiny room. The only furniture in that room consisted of two shabby old double beds. They had nothing else, and it was clear that there was very little food in the place, never mind furniture. It emerged that the father had murdered this little boy's mother about a month after we had left on the last trip and the child was distraught. He had lost not only his mother but also his father overnight.

The uncle showed us the horrific photos of this poor woman lying dead in her coffin, still showing the injuries from where the father had beaten her to a pulp and left her with horrific bruises and scarring. After he killed her, he then fled the country and had not been seen since. The family had taken the children in to avoid them being split up for good and sent to orphanages.

We told this man that we wanted to take the little boy to Ireland for a break. He cried and begged us not to take him away. It took us some time to convince the man that it was only for a short holiday and that he would be well cared for and staying with a good family. It was very hard for him to understand, and he was right to be suspicious of these strangers arriving to take away a child, but we reassured him. He eventually realized that the break might be good for the little lad and so he finally agreed to let him go, begging us to make sure that he'd be OK and that we'd bring him back. It was a very sad situation. We just prayed that Josef would make the trip the next time around, which he did, thank God, and he had a great time. It was exactly what he needed, having gone through hell and back at home.

But many children at the time were deprived of trips away for a number of reasons, such as if the people in the orphanage took a dislike to them, or if they'd been misbehaving. The flights would be fully paid for and everything in place – visas, passports, letters, etc. – and yet on the day they were due to travel, the orphanage might decide, for some unknown reason, not to send them. The guest family would be none the wiser. They would have everything laid out for the child and would have made the trip all the way up to Dublin to pick them up at the airport, but the child just wouldn't arrive. No reason would be given and the family would be left wondering what had happened.

The communication was deplorable. This would have happened sometimes for the most trivial of things. However, if Andreea, for example, had done something to annoy the staff at the orphanage, there was no way they'd have stopped her going, because they knew that if they crossed the likes of myself or one of the other organizers, then there was a price for them to pay and they could not risk losing some of the aid they'd get from us. Romania is definitely a country where money talks.

The trips to some of these orphanages would truly open your eyes. Over the years I have been to establishments in Fagaras, Rupea, Victoria and Codlea. In Fagaras we could drop in at any time of the day or night and things would always be the same. There was no big clean-up for visitors, no cover-up for the foreigners coming in; what you saw was what you got with young Doina, who ran the home. But when it came to the other orphanages, it was made clear to us that we had to ring in advance to say we were on our way. In Codlea it was fine to call at 7 in the morning or at any time of any day and there was never an issue; but that later changed and it became just like the rest of them. We had to alert them in advance, and within minutes things were being cleaned up in anticipation of the foreigners arriving.

When we'd call Doina, food would be laid out to greet us and thank us for all our help. The bread was absolutely gorgeous and they would have a tray of fried eggs sitting there waiting for us. Doina used to bring in a bottle of homemade 'rocket fuel' to us, called *rachiu*, and it was bloody lethal. It was more potent than poteen and you'd be on your ear with it in no time. But it was always given to us as a thank-you gesture for all we were doing for them.

As we sat there drinking, Doina would be running in and out, answering the phone in her office. Every time the phone rang, these little faces would pop around the doorframe with begging eyes. We'd throw the eggs into the bread and hand it out to them and they'd be delighted with themselves. As soon as they'd hear Doina coming back in, they'd run off, stuffing their faces with the sandwiches. By the time Doina got back to us, the plates would be clear. She would look at us in shock, wondering how we ate everything so quickly, but as we cleared the plates she'd have them filled up again and we'd leave it all there until the phone rang again and the kids arrived back at the door for second helpings. She never had a clue what was going on. We were just delighted to see them all running off waving in thanks with their cheeks stuffed to capacity with bread and eggs. It must have been two years before I told her what we had been doing, and when I did she laughed her head off.

There were about 100 children in each orphanage. I eventually found out that most of these children weren't orphans at all. Some of them were children who came from poor families and were sent into the home because their parents couldn't afford to keep them, but in some cases young kids were just thrown into these places because they simply weren't wanted. Their families could have been driving around in Mercedes or BMWs and their kids just abandoned so they could live their lives with no worries about looking after a family.

I got to know one young girl very well, who didn't get to meet her mother until she was 18 years old – old enough to work. Only then did her mother suddenly appear at the orphanage gates to take her off home, because she could now finally earn some money. The problem we had with fundraising was that we never really knew who was a genuine case and who wasn't. It was simply a chance we had to take because we felt we had to help them all. There was no real way of finding out who was genuine and who wasn't.

The older kids in the orphanages would go to school in the morning, and the younger ones would go in the afternoon. When each group finished up after lessons, they would have to stay indoors and start their homework. In Rupea and Codlea, the gates were locked all day and they couldn't get out, but Fagaras was a bit more lenient and the older ones could go out for a while, as long as they were back by a certain time. If they came back late they would be grounded, so they all knew the consequences. It seemed to work well. But in most of the orphanages the children had no real social life besides mixing with the other kids in school.

The home in Fagaras was only for girls. In Victoria it was all older boys; Rupea also catered solely for girls; but in Codlea there was a mix of both sexes, which meant that siblings didn't have to be split up if they were being cared for. It was good for these kids when they were younger, but when they got that bit older there could be problems with teenage boys chasing teenage girls. The staff had to be on the ball all the time watching them. Staffing was minimal and these teenagers were virtually impossible to control at times.

Because so many families were split up, the orphanages would hold a disco once a month, with each home taking turns to host it. This meant that siblings who had been separated could meet up and chat, which helped them stay in touch. These orphanages were all at least an hour away from one another, so the discos also meant a trip out for at least two groups of children. They all lived for that bit of freedom every four weeks or so.

Other institutions across the country catered for those children labelled as having 'special needs'. For years these establishments were totally neglected and the kids left to exist in dreadful circumstances, with little or no playtime or interaction with others and a severe lack of much-needed medication and specialist help. Unfortunately, sometimes children were sent to these places having been diagnosed as disabled, but in some cases they had no disability whatsoever.

In fact, there was one little girl living in an institution who was classed as being disabled but it emerged years later that she wasn't disabled at all. She was only saved from a horrible life when she was adopted by a family from Northern Ireland, and she is thriving now. All that was wrong with this poor mite was that she was a slow learner, but she was thrown into the institution and made out to have a severe disability, which meant she couldn't mix with 'normal' children of her own age. She was a very lucky child because she could still be living there today, with no hope of an escape, only for the Irish woman who recognized something in her and took her in. She was one of the lucky ones.

There have been a lot of families in Northern Ireland who have successfully adopted children from Romania, but the authorities there put a stop to inter-country adoptions back in 2004, stopping so many wee ones from having a better chance in life. The Romanian authorities, in my view, don't seem to care about these children and it's very hard for me to accept. Most of these poor unfortunates live in cramped dormitories, sleeping in bunk beds on dirty sheets and blankets, with no comforts whatsoever. Now, thanks to their government, they are deprived of any hope of a better future.

Many of these kids don't even get to go out on field trips. In Fagaras for example, they had a little run-down minibus, on its last legs, but they couldn't even afford the fuel for the trips out, never mind what it would cost to pay the driver. They got one fill-up of fuel per month as part of their rations, and when that was gone it was gone. If a child got sick during the night and there was no fuel in the minibus to get them to the hospital, it was just tough luck.

I knew what was needed and I knew the price of cars in Romania, so I told Doina that I would do my best to raise some funds to help them get a car that wouldn't break down every other day and that would last them a few years and not eat up the fuel. I wasn't making her any promises, because I wouldn't promise her something unless I knew I could fulfil it.

When I got back home, a few of us organized a couple of fundraising events to bring in the cash. Seamus and Brian Lunney, Aidan McCrossan, myself and a few others went down to John Street in Omagh, at the crossroads outside Sally O'Brien's bar, and we walked up and down the street with buckets getting spare change off motorists and passers-by. Brian had a pair of stilts, because he skimmed ceilings for a living, and he stood in the middle of the road on these stilts. He was blocking the whole road, so as we ran around with the buckets, drivers were only too happy to throw us a few bob so they could move on. In

Mena and I on our wedding day

Our wedding day, with both sets of parents

Mrs Slevin

*Mena, with Andreea, in August
1998 – just days before Mena died
in the Omagh bombing*

*Andreea and I on our way to Dublin Airport in 1999, 11 months after
Mena died*

*Best friends: Shauna and Andreea
at Budapest Airport, 2001*

*Doina, behind me, in Romania,
2002*

Maria and her family in Romania, before our relationship started

Raymond Acheson, with baby Iulia,
2001 – Raymond died in 2009

Paula and David on their wedding
day, Scotland, March 2005

Tracey and Mark's wedding day, December 2005

Getting married at Omagh District Council office, October 2005

Shauna, Paula, myself, Maria, Ray and Tracey

My mam and dad with baby Gabriella

PJ and Connie, godparents to Gabriella, with Maria and me at the christening

Maria and Gabriella on holiday in England

Shauna and Iulia

Iulia, Andreea, Nico and Gabriella

Maria, Iulia, Gabriella and me at home in Kelvin Glen

Little Gabriella, aged two in 2008

Gabriella as she started school, 2009

about an hour and a half we raised £1,700. We hadn't planned it weeks in advance or anything like it, we just decided on the spur of the moment to get out there and do something, and it paid off.

A group called Vintage Rally gave us a big dig-out by raising money from local businesses to have a rally in Omagh, where they drove around in vintage tractors and vintage cars, vehicles that would have been used all over Ireland for farming in the 1930s, 1940s and 1950s. We managed to get a massive $7,000, which we changed into $20 bills to bring back over with us. It went down a treat.

Raymond, myself and a couple of the other lads arrived in Fagaras on Easter Monday and unfortunately the banks were closed, as it was an official holiday. They were also closed the following day, so we had to hold on to the cash and pray that nothing would happen to it or us until the Wednesday. With that amount of money in Romania we would have been prime targets to be killed, never mind robbed. On the Wednesday morning we headed straight to the bank in the town, but we hadn't bargained on the fact that they wouldn't have enough Romanian leu in stock to do the transaction. We then headed off to the banks in nearby Brasov. After walking the streets all day, we eventually found a bank at 5:00 p.m. that could do the deal and we walked out the door with 198,500,000 Romanian leu.

In order to complete the transaction I had to sit down and write out every single serial number of every single $20 bill that I had on a sheet of paper. My fingers were aching for a week. We got out of the bank at 5:45 p.m. that day with this big bag of money. By then, the car showroom was closed.

We headed over to the orphanage with the cash to hold until the next morning, but Doina was terrified to take it in case someone got wind and the place was robbed. So I had to sleep that night with millions of this Romanian currency tightly flattened down under my belly, praying to God that I didn't get shot in the head for the cash.

The next morning, bright and early, we headed off and bought two lovely cars, Dacia estates. One went to the orphanage in Codlea and the other one to Fagaras.

I got a call from another orphanage asking us to come up to them before we headed home. We didn't know what they wanted, but it turned out that when the other two groups got the new cars, they had been given one of the old cars. They were delighted and just wanted to thank us personally. They laid out a big meal for us to eat. God forgive me, but it was the most disgusting thing I have ever tasted. They dished up a cold bean soup, and there was white lard stuck solidly around the top of the plate. But we knew we had to eat it, because they had obviously spent a lot of money putting on this spread to thank us and we couldn't leave without being seen to have eaten something. We would have insulted them if we hadn't tried it.

Raymond and myself were sick for two days after that visit, and the other two who had been with us thought it was absolutely hilarious, because they had left us earlier to go off on their own to a nearby restaurant for a nice steak and a few drinks. They'd had a lovely meal. That experience nearly put me off soup for life; it was years before I put a spoon of any sort of soup into my mouth for fear of being sick.

In general, though, once you got used to the food in Romania it was quite nice, and eating out cost little or nothing. We always brought a few people out for dinner on the night before we left. Maria would come with her partner and some of the lads from the orphanage. A meal and drinks for six people wouldn't cost us much more than £10. Yet when our Romanian friends would see the bill, their eyes would shoot open. They were not used to handing out money for meals, but we were only too happy to pay £10 for a lovely meal. To them every penny counted and we understood how they felt. We were just delighted to be able to give them this little treat every now and then. It was the only time they were shown appreciation for the work they did. It meant a lot to them.

In August 2004 I went to Fagaras for a very special occasion. There had been major concerns about the orphanage where Doina was working, because a lap-dancing club had opened right across the road from the entrance and there were fears for the safety of some of the young girls in Doina's care. But thankfully that year a new orphanage farther up the road was officially opened after many years of fundraising and praying. Our group had a big part to play in raising the funds to get this building up and running, and it gave us so much pleasure knowing that we had done as much as we could to kickstart that building.

When I stood there that day and saw the happiness on the faces of so many people, I thought of Mena and how her interest in taking a child in from Romania had helped to make so many changes to the lives of so many people. If she hadn't died, I very much doubt that I would have got involved in any of this work; yet here we were, six years after her death, having helped so many people to adopt children and change their lives for good, and seeing so many children living a happier life in Romania because of the work we had done back home.

The new orphanage was built totally from money raised by Irish people; all the finance came from Ireland and as a thank you they even called the place 'Irish House'. It receives financial support from the Romanian government, but it was our money that built it from start to finish. Thanks to those who donated, the kids in this home are cared for so much better than in most places and their quality of life has improved tenfold.

In other homes in Romania, the children have to leave once they turn 18, whether they can survive on their own or not; in Irish House, if you are 18 and need help to get sorted in the outside world, the place is there for you until such time as you can survive on your own two feet. You are a lucky child in Romania if you end up there, because you can be sure that you will be well looked after.

It's such a great feeling knowing that there is something to show for what everyone contributed to. It was great to take photos of the work done and show them back home to some of the people who had handed over their hard-earned cash to help those less fortunate. So many people helped us raise cash over the years, helping to ease the plight of others.

As I looked around that day, I thought back to my own childhood. When I was a teenager in the 1970s, my father had an accident in the quarry where he was working. He was sick for so long that we were left with nothing to eat in the house. There were six of us back then – my sister hadn't been born yet – and we would sit around as Mammy cut the mouldy crust off the bread so we could eat the soft bit in the middle of it. She would wait every morning for the postman to arrive, praying he was going to deliver the 'sick money', a state benefit. On the mornings when he didn't arrive, she would hold her head in her hands and cry her eyes out. It would break my heart.

Mammy had a little insurance policy worth very little at the time, but she was waiting for it to come through as well. Until it was sorted, she would get her groceries 'on tick' in a local shop and the owner would write everything into his little book until the time came for us to clear the bill. But when my father took sick, Mammy found it very hard to get by and so the bill was running up and up all the time, until it eventually got to about £50, which was a hell of a lot of money at that time.

One day, when I was about 15, I came in and found my mother sobbing her heart out at the kitchen table. I knew that things must have been really bad. She wiped her face and straightened herself up when I came in. She asked me to go to the shop for a couple of bits and pieces. When I got there, I ordered what she had asked for. In front of a packed shop, Pat Kane wrote it down and threw the book onto the counter to me, open for all to see. I won't forget that day as long as I live. As I cycled home, I swore that as soon as that policy came through, the first thing I was going to do was to cycle down to that shop to pay that bastard off, because I could see the pleasure he got that day out of embarrassing my poor mother in front of all her neighbours.

We had gone through the worst times of our lives and there was no one to help us out; yet that man was sneering at us. So, when the cheque came through the door and my mother cashed it, I got great pleasure in going down to the shop, throwing the money at him and telling him to shove it up his arse.

That is probably why I can relate so much to these poor people in Romania, who have no one there to help them. I look at some of the parents and I know they would do anything they could to change their children's lives, but they just don't have the power to make those changes and no one seems to care.

People forget that many of our own parents or grandparents went through hell and back when they were growing up. It's only for the grace of God that we didn't end up the same way. We have an awful lot to be grateful for nowadays. I sometimes think that if every person who could afford to sponsored one family for just £4 a month, there would be very little poverty in the world today. If we all did our little bit, we could change this world forever.

Chapter 6

Life in Romania

My trips back and forth over the years resulted in me seeing many parts of Romania. It is a truly beautiful country. It is like Ireland was 50 or 60 years ago. The people have a very simple life. At the fairs you can buy anything from nettle leaves to chickens or cows. These fairs take place in fields in the middle of the countryside and people come from miles around to get a bargain. They all stand around haggling and when the deal is done, they spit on their palms, shake hands and off they go together for a drink. Just walking about the marketplace would open your eyes. People have very little and they always want to get the best deal for the little they have.

The thing that scared me most on my trips there was driving at night in the dark. To start with, a lot of the cars in some of the more impoverished areas have holes all over them; when you look down at the floor, you might be looking straight out onto the road. I was petrified in these cars because many Romanians are dreadful drivers and as you come around the corners in the dark, you never know what could be facing you. I've seen horses and carts and battered-up tractors coming at us on the wrong side of the road when we least expected it, forcing us to swerve as fast as we could. They take the carts out at night to deliver hay and corn, and they drive as if they're the only ones around.

I remember getting a lift into Fagaras one time and by the time I got there I thought my legs had been cut off at the knees. I had no feeling whatsoever from the knee down. There was a freezing cold wind blowing up from the floor of the car which had cut the circulation off from my knees down. I couldn't walk when we pulled up, but the driver was so used to this that he didn't even bat an eyelid. He just watched as I staggered out of the car and into the hotel.

On another trip, we started off on our journey to the hotel and about 30 km into the drive the car started to chuck and splutter and then it just suddenly stopped. Without a word, the driver pulled in and jumped out. Up came the bonnet and he screwed the carburettor down a bit, blew the jets out and on we went again. We stopped about ten times on that trip, and each time he pulled up the bonnet and did the same thing again, with not a word said to us. It took us six or seven hours to do a journey that should have taken four.

On that particular occasion we were driving over mountains in deep snow on treacherous roads. As I looked down at my feet all I could see was a blanket of white with pieces of ice splashing up into the car as we sped along. We were lucky to make it there in one piece. But you knew that you were taking your life in your hands on these journeys and you just had to put up with it and keep your fingers crossed that at some stage you'd eventually get there alive. And, thank God, we always did.

Our first trip truly opened our eyes to the plight of the Romanians: people who were the salt of the earth and would spend their last penny to welcome a foreign guest.

Bucharest is a beautiful city, but there are little children living in the sewers who sleep every night in the excrement of thousands of people. These youngsters sniff glue at night to help them sleep, yet no one seems to care. The Romanian government don't want to know and it's all covered up, brushed under the carpet so that the 'civilized' people in the Western world don't hear about it, but it's there and it's not going away. It's a horrific situation and I often think, there but for the grace of God go I.

In places like Fagaras some Roma gypsy children have their limbs tied up at birth and left like that right through their childhood to disfigure them so that when they get older they can make more money begging from people who may feel sympathy for them. This is fairly common over there and most people turn a blind eye. Kids as young as three can be seen standing at the traffic lights begging in the middle of a busy road, wearing nothing but a wee pair of pants and a vest in the freezing cold. These kids will get as much as they can from motorists and passers-by, and then you'll see them run over to their mothers, who have been hiding in a ditch, and handing everything over to them.

There are gangs operating these begging trips all year round and making a small fortune from these poor young ones. Your heart would bleed for them, but there is nothing you can do for them, because they won't get a penny of what you give them; your money just goes straight to the fraudsters. Yet people fall for it all the time, especially tourists.

Instead of giving people money over there to get what they need, we would go to the big shopping centres where you can buy anything from nettle leaves to bathroom suites, and we'd stock up for them. We sometimes spent £1,000 in these places and then distributed it all out to those who needed it in the orphanages.

On one occasion we bought a few trolley-loads of food, including a stack of beef, all sorts of drinks, bread, milk, 20 trays of eggs, everything they could possibly have needed. We brought it all to the orphanage in Codlea at 8:00 p.m. that evening and we didn't get out of it until midnight. The man in charge counted every single egg, every banana, every apple – hundreds of pounds' worth of food had to be counted out item by item and written down in a book. He wanted to make sure that whatever we handed over he could account for the following day; if anything had gone missing, then he wanted to be able to pinpoint it and find out where the spare egg or banana went.

When we went up to the orphanage in Fagaras I said to the man in charge, 'You have got exactly the same as what we handed into Codlea, so for Jaysus' sake just write it down, 'cos we're not counting it all again.' They were all delighted with their big delivery and it meant that they could save that few bob on food to put towards something else for the kids.

We didn't bring clothes on our trips – they would go in the van on an annual run – but I remember one day Shauna went out and bought some clothes for a beautiful little girl whom we got to know from begging on the street. The poor child was filthy dirty and clearly starved, but Shauna took her into the hotel, washed her, combed her hair and put the lovely new clothes on her. She looked like a little doll by the time Shauna had finished with her. The child was delighted with herself as she walked back out onto the street. But the very next day, that child was back in her rags, filthy dirty and begging. We heard later that her mother had gone back down to the market to sell the clothes and shoes back. We learned the hard way not to do anything like that again. Instead, if we saw a child in a bad way, we'd take them for a pizza, because we knew the parents wouldn't get anything from that act of kindness.

Shauna was great on these trips. She had come with us every year and her help was invaluable, especially with the younger kids.

On each trip to Romania, we would normally arrive at the hotel at around 2:00 in the morning. As soon as we got there, word would get around that the tourists were in. Within minutes, children would be at the door of the place, in their droves, begging. I remember on one occasion a kid followed us around the town all day and all night, begging and calling out, 'Mr Money, Mr Money'. Our heads were done in with him, so at one stage Raymond Acheson, who was with me on the trip, turned around and said, 'Ah, Mr Money, feck off,' and sure the poor young fella continued following us around the streets for hours shouting, 'Money please, Mr Feck Off.' It was sad and hilarious at the same time.

In fairness, for all the horrific things we saw over the years and all the situations we witnessed, we always had some happy times as well on these visits. Some of that, it has to be said, was to do with the fact that the drink was so cheap. When we weren't going around visiting the orphanages and delivering food, we would be in a pub having a few scoops and a bit of craic. If we didn't have that 'down time', we'd have been coming back in a depressed state. You always need to get away for a while from the reality of what is happening in these places or you would crack up. There is only so much we can all do to help these children and their families, and having a few hours away from it all gives you time to de-stress, unwind and start again the next day.

On one trip we stayed in a rundown hotel in Fagaras. It was a skip, with filthy rooms and shared toilets, the usual hole in the floor. A group of lads were over on this particular visit, along with Shauna and myself. Another lady who came with us, Gwen Annies, went off to Rupea to stay with a little girl she was adopting called Helena. Unfortunately, we drank more than ever before on this visit. I was disgusted with how things turned out, because we got so scuttered on Romanian beer that we lost the run of ourselves. We did all the shopping and delivered it to the orphanage as planned, but we didn't get half the things done that we had intended. I am embarrassed to admit this, and we should have been ashamed of ourselves. On this occasion we agreed not to drink in the daytime and just to get on with things before we wound down.

Gwen got everything in place in Rupea to start her adoption process on that trip. Her adopted daughter Helena, who was about 15 back then and is in her twenties now, is still living in Northern Ireland and doing very well.

However, on that trip we had a very hairy moment. Andreea was still in the orphanage at that time, but we had taken her out to stay with us in the hotel nearby. She was sleeping in with Shauna. Doina knew we could be trusted, which is why she allowed her to stay with us. I had noticed from the day we arrived that the hotel was very quiet in the day, but it suddenly came alive at night – and not with the entertainment you'd expect. It turned out that they were running a brothel.

On the third or fourth night there, I woke up in the early hours of the morning to hear a commotion outside. I jumped up out of the bed and ran out to find a big man dragging Andreea down the stairs to throw her out of the hotel. Shauna was screaming at him to stop, so I grabbed hold of him and grabbed hold of Andreea. I started to scream at the top of my voice, telling him I'd kill him if he didn't let her go. With that, he pulled a gun on me and put it to my head. I didn't know whether he was going to shoot me or not, but I stood my ground and continued to scream at him to let her go. I could feel the barrel of the gun at my head and I knew that I was taking a huge chance even trying to argue with him, but he had both children in his grasp and I wasn't giving up. He understood my English well enough as I started to shout louder and louder. Then, all of a sudden, he released his grip and Shauna dragged Andreea back into the bedroom as he walked away.

The poor girls were in an awful state and we moved out that very day. We reckoned he did it because he knew she was from the orphanage and he didn't want her to give the game away about what was happening in the rooms. In his head, if he threw her out she'd be afraid to say anything to anyone. But you have to stand up to these pimps, because they are just out to make money and will stop at nothing to make sure their business is protected. Needless to say, we never went back to that place again.

Chapter 7

Maria

As I got to know Maria a bit better, we began to visit her home for the odd cup of tea or a bit of dinner when we were in Romania. We would head up to her flat, and she was hospitable to everyone. We all knew that making a meal for us could well have put her into debt, but that is how the Romanian people are: they love to look after visitors. If we were to worry about the cost and snub her, she would have been very upset. She was delighted about what we were doing for Andreea and understood that we only had her best interests at heart.

Shauna came with me on most trips and she always visited Maria. They got on very well. This made things easier when it came to organizing further holidays for the girls, both Andreea and Nicoletta. Maria was picking up the odd English word and her niece could speak English as well, so the language wasn't a huge barrier. No matter what we had to say, for some reason we all understood each other.

On our second trip to Romania, in March 2000, I was very eager to see Maria again. In fact, I felt like a teenager; I had butterflies in my stomach just with the thought of meeting up with her and being in her company again. I knew she was in a relationship and she seemed to be happy, but there was something there between us – as far as I was concerned anyway – and I was hoping that it wasn't all in my head.

I never said anything to my own family or to Andreea, but I had decided to ask Maria to come over to Northern Ireland with the two girls in October of that year so that she could see what the place was like for herself. I could see how hard it was for her to get by in her tiny little flat and I wanted her to have a taste of what it could be like if at any time she wanted to move out of Romania. I suppose I was also being selfish, hoping that she might someday tell me she had feelings for me as well and that we might eventually have some sort of relationship. Seeing where I lived, I thought, might help her to come to that decision. I was riddled with guilt over how I was feeling, but I knew that no matter how hard I tried, I just couldn't get her out of my mind. So, on that visit I planned to ask her how she would feel about a holiday with the girls in October.

Maria arrived over to the hotel to meet us the day after we arrived. My stomach turned when I noticed that she was pregnant. Initially she said nothing, but it was very obvious to everyone. In my mind, that was the start of the end. I had met her partner, Ovideo, who seemed like a lovely man, but I was sick when I realized that she was going to have a baby with him. I couldn't bear to think about him being with her, never mind the fact that she was now pregnant with his child. So, the idea of asking her to come back home to our place went out the window there and then.

She eventually told us that the baby was due sometime in July. She was over the moon. There was no way that I could interfere in her relationship now, and I could see that she was truly settling down with her partner. The baby would definitely seal the relationship between herself and Ovideo, as it would be their first child together as a couple. Andreea and Nicoletta's father had gone off the scene years earlier and Maria had only recently set up with Ovideo. I had to accept that she had moved on, and try to get on with it as best I could.

Maria told me that she would call the child Kevin if it was a boy and if it was a girl she would give her the second name of Mena, in appreciation of what Mena's legacy had meant to her and her family. She knew that, had it not been for Mena wanting to take a Romanian child, we would never have met and her two eldest children would probably still be in the orphanage. I was very touched by that. On 12 July 2000, Maria gave birth to a beautiful little girl. She called her Iulia Mena.

Maria told us that she was planning to get married before the baby was born, but when she heard we were coming back in October, she delayed the ceremony and asked me to be her best man. I was knocked for six by this, but I couldn't let people see that I didn't want them to get married. I couldn't refuse to act as best man. I accepted immediately and said I'd love to do it. I could see that she was delighted. To be honest, my heart was broken and I felt sick at the thought of standing there and seeing this woman, whom I had fallen head over heels in love with, marry another man. But I had to do it, not just for Maria but for Andreea and Nicoletta.

I left after that March 2000 trip feeling gutted. Maria and Ovideo looked so excited and I had to appear to be as happy as they were. The truth of it was that I couldn't have felt worse. But I knew that I had to put my own personal feelings to the back of my mind, and that I would have to do it no matter what.

All the lads who travelled back and forth with me over the years were also invited to the wedding, because they knew we would all be back together on that trip to visit the orphanages. So, that day in October, they all went along.

On the night before the wedding we all got absolutely slaughtered; I think I drank enough to keep me drunk for six months on that one night, and I now know that I used the drink to cover up my emotions. But on the day of the wedding itself I never let a sup pass my lips. I went straight from morning to night without a taste of liquor, and that was a first for me in a long time. When I was with Mena I had a few every now and then, but my drinking simply spiralled out of control after I lost her and it was hard to stop myself sometimes, especially when I was with a group who also loved their booze.

But I knew that if I'd had a few drinks I wouldn't have been fit for the flight home later that night. Ideally we should have flown home the next day, but some of the lads had to go back to work and so we had no choice but to book a flight for that night. I remember looking at one of the lads in the church that day. He swayed back and forth after a whole night of binge drinking. He looked like he was going to collapse at any minute; he was absolutely snow-white and I knew that if the clergyman didn't stop talking, he would be taken away in an ambulance.

A Romanian wedding is nothing like a wedding ceremony in Ireland, where everybody is in and out in 45 minutes. This went on for over an hour and a half. The priest waffled on and on, and of course it was all in Romanian so we couldn't make head nor tail of it. All we could do was sit there and look interested. It was quite funny.

At one stage everyone suddenly turned around and started to stare over at me. I hadn't a clue what was going on until they all started to smile and then clap. I could feel myself getting redder and redder, because I hadn't a clue what was happening. It turned out that the priest was telling everyone how grateful Maria was to me for helping her family and how things would never have been as they were had I not taken Andreea on holiday and then come over with a plan to adopt her. Although I was mortified with everyone looking at me, whispering and pointing, I was secretly delighted that Maria had thought to highlight this on that particular day. It made me feel very special.

They have the strangest but most brilliant wedding ceremony in Romania. Before you even get to the church, the celebrations begin. At the bride's flat, the front door is covered from top to bottom in palm leaves, flowers of every colour and a variety of coloured balloons. The bride's godfather and godmother come to the house before she leaves and pin flowers to her dress, giving her a little envelope with a few bob in it. All the neighbours visit the house to see what the bride looks like and wish her all the best for the future, but to get out again they have to put money in a bucket as a present. It could be the equivalent of a pound or a fiver, but you have to give something. It's a good luck gift for the bride and groom.

At the church everyone dances around and around in circles and prays that the couple will be blessed. I'd had my fill of drink the night before, as I said, and I was truly paying the price at this stage, as my stomach was in an awful state. I thought that I'd throw up at any minute. But I had to go on dancing with them, because I was the best man. All I could do was to pray for the best, that I wouldn't make a show of myself.

During the ceremony we all had to eat a little biscuit dipped in honey, and drink from the wine chalice. The thought of swallowing anything, never mind a biscuit dipped in honey, made me feel sick. Then, in another tradition, the bride or groom has to kick a jug of holy water outside the chapel. If the wife smashes it, then the saying goes that her next baby will be a little girl; if the man kicks and breaks it, then they'll have a baby boy. Lo and behold, it was Maria who smashed the jug.

As they left the church, the guests threw rice and confetti over them to shower them with wealth and happiness, just like in Ireland. Then we headed off to the restaurant. There were about 20 of us in total. The tradition is that, after the dinner and the first dance, someone comes up to the bride out of the blue and 'kidnaps' her. The best man has to run through the streets to find her and bring her back.

I knew nothing about this tradition. So, when Maria was snatched away, I didn't have a clue what was going on. For all I knew she could have been genuinely kidnapped. I didn't know what was happening when they all started to scream that Maria had been taken. The only giveaway was that everyone was laughing and joking, so I knew that, whatever it was, it was meant to be funny.

So the bride was gone and it was my job to find her. It's a mad game and at that stage I was very grateful that I hadn't succumbed to 'the hair of the dog' and gone on a binge, because I was running around the place like an idiot trying to find her. This game goes on all day and all night, because when she eventually gets back someone else robs her or her veil and you have to get the bride or the veil back again for cash. All of this cash is not given to the newlyweds as you'd expect – it goes to the person who kidnapped her, so everyone is planning how to get her out of the restaurant without being seen. It's a way of people making a few bob on the day, so they probably plan their kidnap for months in advance. Looking back on it, the whole thing is quite funny and all adds to the atmosphere of the day.

The first time Maria was kidnapped it was by a friend of hers. Someone finally tipped me off as to who had taken her and I had to go to this girl's house to get her back. Then she was kidnapped again later that night and I had to race off again to try and get her back. It was a mad experience but it was a great bit of craic. I don't know how much I paid that night to get her back; it was only something like £40 sterling, but a lot of money in Romania.

Of course, when we arrived back at the restaurant everyone was dancing around the room, hyper, waiting to see if we had got her back and how much we'd had to pay. It's the best man's responsibility before midnight to hand over the cash, but once the clock hits 12 the responsibility falls on the new husband, so I was delighted that I had to leave early to catch a plane or I'd have been fleeced!

If I hadn't been so upset at the events of the day, at Maria marrying this man, I would have to say it was a great experience to see how things are done in Romania. I left that night feeling devastated that Maria was now married, but we'd had a great day. I had played my part as I had agreed that day and kept my promise to Maria, but it broke my heart.

All I wanted to do then was to get on that plane home and conk out. We were all shattered. It was a four-and-a-half-hour drive from Fagaras to the airport in Bucharest. Then we had to wait for two hours to board and then face the long flight home, stopping off in Amsterdam as there were no direct flights at that time to Belfast.

All the way to the airport I kept thinking that it was going to be harder to go back now that I knew there was no hope of a future with this woman. I knew I still had so much work to do with the orphanages, but I didn't honestly know how I was going to get through it.

I spoke to Maria over the phone a few times in the months that followed and she seemed to be very happy. I promised her that I'd be over at Easter the following year. Despite my reservations, I fulfilled that promise. I thought about her so often in the months coming up to that trip. It was getting harder and harder for me to accept that I would never be with her. But that was life.

On this trip in 2001, though, I did what I had to do. I did my usual work with the orphanages and I got on with things as best I could. I stayed with Maria and Ovideo for the few days, though it was difficult for me to accept that they would head off at night into bed and I'd be there on my own. I could see that things weren't as rosy as I'd thought, though, and from the odd glance I got from Maria I somehow still felt that she might have had feelings for me. But again I ignored my own thoughts and got on with things.

This happened on all of my visits. In 2002 and 2003 I could see their relationship deteriorating further, and it definitely didn't appear to be a happy-ever-after union. Each time I visited, it seemed to be worse. Ovideo and Maria were clearly just hanging on to their relationship by a thread, and it looked as though Maria was struggling to get by on a daily basis. She never said anything to me, but you would have had to be a fool not to notice.

By this stage, Andreea was coming over occasionally on what I thought were two-week visas. I realized later that the visas were actually for six months. Once I copped onto that she stayed over for longer periods on each trip. They loved where we lived and they never wanted to go back anyway. Eventually Andreea came over to live with us in Omagh. She came over for good in December 2004. It took a lot of effort to organize, a lot of red tape to get through, a lot of phone calls made and I spent a lot of money on trips back and forth, but I finally managed to get her a student visa so that she could further her education back with us in Northern Ireland. She started at Omagh College of Further Education in September 2005, studying beauty therapy. When she qualified in that, she went on to study hairdressing.

Maria was initially upset, like any mother would be, to see her child leave, but she knew that Andreea was in safe hands and that we would take care of her, so in the end she said that she was happy for her to head off. I had told Maria that I would also work at getting Nicoletta a visa so she could also benefit from a better education, and she was very grateful. It also made things a bit easier for her to manage with just the one child in Romania to look after, to feed and clothe. Of course the girls were delighted with coming to live in Northern Ireland.

Ovideo and Maria were hardly talking to each other by this stage. It wasn't a happy home and I knew how stressful it must be for the whole family, but of course I couldn't get involved. In 2003, Shauna, Nico and Andreea went off to Ibiza on holiday and Nico phoned me to say that Maria was in trouble and she had no money for food for Iulia. I knew that things must have been bad, because neither the girls nor Maria had ever asked for money to be sent over before. She asked me if I would send some money over to Maria, and I was only too happy to do so. Maria never asked me for a penny because she had her pride. I could tell that Maria was clearly unhappy, but she still said nothing to me when we spoke on the phone. I knew the way she was thinking was that she had made her bed and she now had to sleep in it.

I went out at Easter 2004 for the opening of the new orphanage in Fagaras, and I think Maria struggled not to tell me how bad things were, as I was staying with herself and Ovideo in the flat on this visit, along with Andreea. I thought she was going to break a few times, but I think she just couldn't get the words out. On that trip in 2004 I did my best to act normally, but it was very hard.

I was always watching out for signs from Maria that she had feelings for me; always living in the hope that there still could be some light there. I found out later that she had said to Nico that year that she would like to be with me, but she thought I wouldn't be interested in her. She thought she wasn't good enough for me. Little did she know how I had felt from day one, how I was in love with her from the moment I saw her standing in the freezing cold outside that orphanage in Fagaras. We were both foolishly thinking that the other person couldn't be interested in a relationship, yet we were both madly in love and trying desperately to fight our feelings.

Nico later told me that, as the eldest child, she could see how we both felt about each other from very early on in our friendship. She said she knew that her mother had feelings for me but she, Nico, also thought it mightn't work at the beginning because of the different cultures and the language barrier, but she said she always felt in her heart that we would end up together some day.

That Easter of 2004 as I travelled home on the plane, I made my mind up once and for all to stop the trips. Just seeing Maria each time was breaking my heart. Looking at her, knowing that I could never be with her and feeling guilty about what my own family would think was eating me up. Not only had I to deal with how the girls would feel, but I was also trying to convince myself that, if anything did happen between us, Mena would be OK with everything. I felt so eaten up with guilt for how everyone else would feel, and all of these feelings were stopping me from just accepting that some day I might be lucky enough to find love for the second time.

I said goodbye to Maria that week knowing in my heart that this was it; this was probably the last time I would ever see her again. I had a sickening feeling in my stomach, as if someone had died, and I was at my lowest ebb. I truly felt that there was nothing really to go on for. There was no reason to go back to Romania. I knew that I had done my best and there was nothing more I could do to change things. I felt I was only kidding myself, thinking this relationship had any future at all.

I could do what I had to do back home to raise as much money as I could for the orphanages. I had the girls in education in Northern Ireland, knowing they would have better prospects now than they could ever have had back in their homeland. I was happy that I had managed to see the new orphanage open and know that things would be a little better, at least for some children, in Romania.

But that journey home was the worst trip of my life. No one could help me this time. As usual it was the drink that numbed things; numbed the pain and the heartbreak. I had lost Mena and I could never have Maria. But it was out of my hands and I just had to live with it.

Chapter 8

The Letter

I knew that I wouldn't be able to face Maria again, knowing that she was now settled and trying to get on with her own life. At the same time, I suspected that she might have had feelings for me in the months prior to her marriage, because I had sometimes caught her looking at me in a certain way and then sheepishly turning away when our eyes met. There were many little signs that I thought I was seeing, but after the wedding I decided that it must simply have been my imagination playing tricks on me. I wasn't going to put myself through any more torture. If she was really trying to repair her marriage, then I had to let her get on with her life. Andreea and Nicoletta came back with me on the plane. I was very quiet. They knew there was something wrong – you would have to have been a fool not to see it – but they said nothing to me, nor I to them.

I tried to get on with my life back home as best I could, but it wasn't easy. Every afternoon at 2 o'clock Irish time, if the girls were in the house, I would say to them, 'Your mammy would be home from work now,' as it would have been 4 o'clock in Romania. I clock-watched all the time, and every hour I would look and wonder what Maria was up to at that stage. My days and nights were filled with thinking about her. I still felt hugely guilty about these thoughts, but I couldn't control them.

Then, out of the blue, in November 2004 I got a letter from Romania. I knew it was from Maria. It was a letter within a letter; there was one for Nicoletta and inside that was one for me. I sat down and started to read it. It was in broken English, written by her niece, and the gist of it was that Maria was very unhappy. She was splitting up with her husband and she wanted me to know that she had feelings for me.

She put all her cards on the table. She said that she missed me and she hoped that her letter would not change our relationship, as she still wanted us to be friends. She said that she appreciated all I had done for her and her children and that I would never realize how much I meant to her. She didn't think that I had any feelings for her. At the end, she said that if she was wrong to think like this, then she was sorry.

But of course, I *did* have feelings for her; I had been eaten up inside thinking about her for years. I must have read that letter a hundred times. It took a long time for it to sink in, and my feelings were all over the place. However, I didn't want to open up a can of worms and make things worse for everyone by just jumping on a plane and flying off to Romania. I wanted to do that, there and then, but I knew I couldn't because it would have caused uproar at home.

As soon as it all sank in, I rang Maria immediately and we had a very long chat. I told her that I felt exactly the same about her. I didn't go into much detail on the phone but I let her know that I wanted to be with her but that I couldn't go back to Romania until she and Ovideo had sorted everything out. I explained that I would never want to be responsible for breaking up a marriage and I hoped that that wasn't the case. I asked her to be certain she was doing the right thing before she did anything rash. I knew at the back of it that Maria just wasn't happy with him.

After a lot of heart-to-heart talking, she agreed that it would be best if I waited a while until she had sorted herself out. I said I would go over the following Easter, 2005, if things were still the same and she still wanted me.

Maria did try to salvage her marriage, and she even offered Ovideo another chance to save their relationship, but he had also had enough and agreed that things were irreparable between them. I have to be honest and say that I was so happy that things had come to an end between them. I felt sorry for Ovideo, but I knew he wasn't happy either, so this made it easier for me.

In the meantime, I spoke to Maria every day. My phone bills were sky-high, but just to hear her voice each day lifted my spirits. I was in a house on my own all of the time – the kids were never there; they had their own lives to lead – and I felt at times that I would crack up, but knowing that I could pick up the phone and call her without feeling guilty made such a difference.

Nico was the only one who knew what was happening. She knew that her mother had feelings for me right from the beginning, and when the letter arrived she was delighted. She could instantly see how my humour changed. I didn't say anything to anyone else, not even my own kids, but I hoped that they would eventually understand and be happy for me. I also hoped that Mena would be OK with it. I suppose that was my biggest concern.

Then one day, while I was talking to Maria on the phone, my emotions took over and I just blurted it out: 'Will you marry me?' As I said it, I felt a rush of anxiety. I thought I might have pushed things a little too much, let my feelings take over and my heart rule my head. But she just laughed and said 'Yes' – straight out, no pause for thought and no asking for a bit more time. When I put down the phone I was so full of energy, so happy, that I could have run a marathon. She made me the happiest man in the world and I knew that no one could stop us being together. It was meant to be.

I remember how delighted I was that day, knowing that this woman truly loved me. I trusted her and somehow I knew, deep down, that we were going to last.

I also knew that I would be the talk of the place once it got out. There would be a lot of people ready to slam me, thinking that this gorgeous foreign woman was only after a visa and a better life, but I no longer cared what anyone else thought. I knew what was best for me, and I knew that now was the time to start moving on with my life. To be honest, I felt I was due a bit of happiness. I had gone through enough heartache over the years, and I was so happy that there seemed to be a light at the end of what had been a very dark tunnel. I was just absolutely thrilled that this loving, caring woman wanted to marry me.

I thought about Mena a lot. I felt that in a strange way Mena was there with me when I blurted out my proposal, and that she was giving me her blessing.

I decided, despite my relief and happiness, that I would keep it to myself for the time being and tell no one what had happened. There was no point in causing any friction within the family until everything was sorted and I'd had time to talk to Maria face to face.

After that call, things seemed to get much easier for both of us. Speaking every day gave us both something to look forward to and it seemed all our other problems were fading away. Nothing else seemed to matter any more. It was as if we knew it was only a matter of time before we would be together.

I didn't travel back to Romania until March 2005, when Maria and Ovideo's divorce came through. In fact, the delay in going back didn't bother me at all because it gave me time to get my head together and to try and make a plan for my trip to Fagaras and Maria's arrival to Ireland.

Just as I had expected, when I announced to my own family that I was going back on my own to visit Maria, the shit well and truly hit the fan. Even Maria's family were unhappy that I was intending to start a relationship with her. I know for a fact that if Andreea had got her hands on that letter first, I would never have seen it, because she was disgusted that her mother wanted to see me and possibly start a new life with me.

Andreea had all of my attention, along with Shauna, and I think she felt that her mammy coming to Northern Ireland would ruin everything. But I couldn't put my life on hold for anyone. I knew that I would get one crack at changing my life, at 50 years of age, and if I didn't take it with both hands and run, it would never come around again. This made a lot of people very unhappy. I believe Shauna felt that if another woman came into my life she would try to replace her mammy, and inevitably I wouldn't give her (Shauna) as much time. But she must have known that no one could, or would, ever replace Mena, and no one would ever make me shun any of my children.

Maria eventually told Ovideo that she had feelings for me and that I would be coming over as usual. To be fair to him, he was brilliant. Another man would have wanted to kill me, even knowing that I had nothing to do with his marriage breaking up. In fact, throughout everything, he was fantastic.

Ovideo was an orphan himself and he had never found out who his own mother was, so he didn't exactly have a great childhood to start off with. I think he appreciated how good I was to all of the kids, even his own little girl, Iulia. He was a good worker and I hold him in the highest respect for how nice he was to me through everything. I wouldn't be married to Maria today if Ovideo, out of the goodness of his heart, didn't do what he did – and I am not talking about divorcing her. He had to sign papers to allow Iulia to leave the country in the first place; and further down the line, he even signed the papers to allow me to adopt Iulia as my own daughter. Not many a man would do that, and I hold him in the highest esteem for it. There are a lot of people out there who wouldn't even think of doing it; they wouldn't do it out of spite. Ovideo could also have asked me for £5,000 up front to make things easier for him as he tried to pick up the pieces in his own life, but he didn't do that either. He helped make everything smooth from day one, with no questions asked.

Iulia's adoption took nearly 20 months to go through, but it didn't affect us because we knew that everything would eventually go according to plan. We had police checks and social workers coming to visit us every month, asking me why I believed I would make a good father to this little girl and how I was going to support her. Endless questions, despite the fact that Iulia had been living with me for three years, since they'd come over in May 2005. Thank God, it eventually all went through in December of 2008, and after all the to-ing and fro-ing it was all over in a matter of minutes in a little courtroom in Omagh town. Despite all of the red tape, the endless interviews and the frustration, we were just delighted that we could finally move on, knowing that this little girl now had stability in her life and I could make them all a bit happier, give them things they never had.

Ovideo has a wee child himself now with another woman, and I hope that he will be happy with his new life. He deserves happiness. He had no brothers, sisters or parents and yet he helped me to get everything sorted to make sure that Maria and Iulia were properly cared for.

If I went out to Romania today and bumped into him, I would have no problem going for a drink with him; there is no animosity between us at all. He knows that I didn't take Maria from him; they just fell apart. I believe that everything happens for a reason and that our lives were mapped out for us from day one. I still miss Mena every single day, but I now know that it was Mena who made all of this happen. I truly believe that she is up there looking down on us and that she is OK with how things have turned out. Call it heavenly intervention if you like, but I believe that Mena has been looking over me all this time. She knows what has been happening and she is happy for me, for us all.

Chapter 9

Planning Our Wedding

When I went back to Romania in March 2005 for the first time after I received that letter, it was amazing. I was scared stiff on the plane going over. My stomach was in my mouth that day. I hadn't been with a woman in seven years and I genuinely didn't know what to do. It was like walking on eggshells.

I wanted to make an entrance and to make Maria proud of me, so I had arrived dressed in a suit, shirt and tie with my head shaved and wearing a pair of cowboy boots. When I stepped off that plane and saw her standing there waiting for me, I felt like I was 16 once more. Maria laughed out loud when she saw me; she thought the clothes were hilarious. Needless to say, it was a long time before I put another suit on!

Still, she was clearly delighted to see me and I was the happiest man in the world. We hugged each other and I gave her a peck on the cheek. I really didn't know what to do and I didn't want to scare her. But it felt absolutely perfect, and I was content for the first time in years.

We went back to the flat and at first I felt very uneasy. All of my other trips saw me sit there while Maria and Ovideo ran around after us. I was always a guest. This time I had to try to relax more, to make myself at home. I wasn't on a working trip; this time I was there for myself. It was an odd experience, but I remember sitting there, looking at Maria and thinking this couldn't be happening. I had never imagined that I could be happy again. After Mena, I had never imagined meeting anyone with whom I could spend the rest of my life, and yet here I was in a strange country, with a woman who spoke very little English, and I was the happiest man in the world.

In broken English, Maria tried to explain what had happened with Ovideo and how she had always had feelings for me. She was very grateful to me for taking care of her children and she kept telling me how my help had changed her life. We had something to eat that night and we chatted as best we could. I felt so at ease with her. Our first kiss was something special. I thought that I would be very uneasy, but I wasn't and I knew there and then that we would last, that this was for real.

We spent our time together on that trip simply getting to know each other better. The broken English didn't seem to be too much of a problem and somehow we got by. It was great to be with her on my own, with no one else around, and we really felt comfortable with each other.

I saw how good a mother Maria was to her baby and I realized how much she missed her two eldest girls. This trip really brought us closer together and we spoke about our future together and how it would all work if she came to live with me in Tyrone. She seemed very excited and I told her that I would have to go back home and start working on how we could get her back to Ireland. She knew that I had to go to Scotland, as

Paula was getting married, and that once I had everything in order I would be back for her.

I had told Paula that I was going back out to Romania and she didn't really ask me any questions. She organized things before I went so that I could head straight back to Omagh after my Romanian trip and then fly to Scotland for the wedding. Unfortunately, before I even got to Romania, the trouble had begun.

The airline tickets that Paula had sorted for me arrived at the house on Creaghmore Road before I got home. When Shauna and Andreea found them, all hell broke loose. They were disgusted that I had made all these plans behind their backs and they were both very unhappy that I hadn't spoken to them about it. Our relationship became very estranged during this time, but they knew that, despite everything, I still loved them all.

I knew they were all feeling aggrieved; I could feel it in the air around the house, and yet no one opened their mouth. It was very uncomfortable at times for me, knowing they were thinking badly of me and saying nothing. But I had to take any chance I could to get my life back on track and try and put everyone else's feelings to the back of my mind.

Very few people wanted me to go to Maria. They all had their own reasons, but no one could change my mind. I think most of them were just worried for me, in case I was making the wrong decision. I knew that I was getting one last chance at happiness and I wasn't going to blow it for anyone. I didn't want to be alone any more. No one realizes, unless they have gone through it themselves, what it is actually like to lose a spouse – your wife, your friend – and to have to try and get on with your life as best you can. It is a nightmare. I knew that I had strong feelings for this woman in Romania who had stolen my heart the very day I first met her. I knew that I had to be selfish myself and put my own feelings first. So I did.

I went to the wedding as planned in Gretna Green. It was the quickest wedding ceremony I have ever been at in my life. Within minutes it was over and we were in the bar. I knew that there was tension with the kids over the return flights, but nothing was said on the day and we all put everything behind us and had a great night.

Despite the coldness of everyone at home and the darting looks I was getting from some people, I returned to Fagaras as planned, intending to stay for six weeks to see how things worked out. Maria came from a totally different background from myself, a different country, a different culture, and of course I knew that I could have been setting myself up for a big fall. What if she never settled in Ireland? What would I do then? She would be coming to a house where the kitchen was as big as her flat. She'd be meeting strange people, speaking a strange language and she might hate it. How would I cope if that happened? How would she cope? My head was wrecked with questions. She would have her children with her, of course, but the rest of her family, her sisters and friends, would not be there. If she felt down or wanted to talk to someone or have a cup of coffee with them, she couldn't. All of this stuff crossed my mind. But being with her somehow made my life feel complete once again.

We spent the next few days talking and planning. I had no choice but to go back to Northern Ireland at some stage, but I asked Maria how she would feel about living there. She knew that moving abroad would give her a whole new life, more chances to provide a better life for her baby girl, but it was still a huge upheaval. She had sisters in Romania, one of whom she saw all the time, and it would be very hard to give up that part of her life. But she said she would love to see what it was like in Tyrone and she didn't mind leaving her family behind if it meant a better life and happiness.

She knew Andreea and Nicoletta loved their new life and she was missing them. There was no way that those girls would ever go back to live in Romania and Maria knew that, so she was only too happy to live with me in a new country.

After days of talking and trying to work out how she would cope in a new country and how she would leave things in Romania, we decided to start the ball rolling. We decided to see how Maria would get on if she came on a holiday visa for six months. It would give her time to see the place and get an idea of what it would be like to live here.

We knew that because of the rules and regulations of the British government we would have to return to Romania, and the plan was to get married back there. But I never bargained for the difficulties I'd encounter trying to get a visa for Maria from Romania which would give her permission just to stay for a holiday. I had to write a letter of invitation asking for the state's permission to have her come over.

I also handed in a letter I had organized from Doina in the orphanage explaining all of the voluntary work I had been doing with them over the years. Knowing that I had an interest in the plight of Romanian children, Doina believed, may have helped them see in the embassy that I wasn't coming over looking for a 'mail-order bride' or anything like that. I had been back and forth to Romania for years before anything started between myself and Maria, despite my own feelings from day one, but there was no way I was visiting their country looking for love. I said in the letter that her daughters were already living with us in Omagh, and also that my two daughters were getting married and both wanted to invite Maria over for the ceremonies. Of course, Paula was already married at that stage and Tracey was getting married in December, so I told a few white lies, but you have to do whatever is necessary to get someone out of Romania. I didn't care if it meant lying; I wanted her to come home with me and that was that.

We had to queue outside the British Embassy in Bucharest at 6 o'clock in the morning, where we were treated like animals, shunted into a corner like a herd of cows. You had to write your name in a book and stand waiting until a boy came out at 9 o'clock and started to hand out numbers. We stood there until about 11, by which time we were drained. As soon as we got inside the doors of the embassy, we were immediately asked to hand over our mobile phones. No matter what question was asked, they blamed the situation on Romania, despite the fact that as soon as we got inside there were signs everywhere telling us that we were now on British soil. We had to pay £100 just to be seen.

I had warned Maria not to speak one word of English. There was a woman in the room who started talking in Romanian and I hadn't a clue what she was saying. Another man at the desk asked me if I spoke Romanian and, when I said that I didn't, he said that we therefore had a problem on our hands as Maria might have a big problem with the language barrier in Omagh. I told him that I had known Maria for a number of years and that we had always managed to communicate.

I told him that I didn't see it as a problem at all. I asked him if he knew anything at all about Northern Ireland and he said that all he knew was that they used to kill one another. My answer to him was, 'You are dead right. And you see the politicians, well, not one of them speaks to the others, the DUP don't speak to the UUP, the UUP don't speak to Sinn Féin, Sinn Féin don't speak to the SDLP, Sinn Féin don't speak to the DUP – so she'll fit in perfectly!' He started to laugh.

I was told to leave the room and they continued to question Maria. When she came out, we were told to come back at 4:00 p.m. So we headed off to a café, where Maria said she'd been told that she had been unsuccessful, but to come back at 4:00 p.m. anyway. I was sick. This had happened before with Andreea – after me waiting all day, she had been refused a visa. So we went back at 4:00 as instructed but I couldn't disguise my disappointment. However, about 20 minutes after we arrived, a man came down with a bundle of passports and one of them was handed to Maria. She had been given the visa. Maria had been playing a joke on me all the time, and she had left me with my heart in my mouth. The relief I felt was amazing, and I just grabbed her into my arms and gave her a big kiss.

Falling in love with Maria brought with it lots of problems, not only with the language barrier but with family, friends, government red tape, the lot. But despite it all, I was the happiest I had been in years. Maria, for her part, was over the moon. She started to plan her trip, saying goodbye to her friends and family, packing up all of her personal belongings. She was very excited about going to Tyrone, but she was also very worried about how other people would treat her and how my family would feel when they all realized we were planning to get married.

I promised her that I wouldn't put any pressure on her and that if she felt it was all too much for her, I would organize tickets for her to go back to Fagaras and we could decide then what to do. She was free to make her own mind up. If it didn't work out in Romania then we would just try something else. I didn't know exactly what we could do, but I was willing to take that chance.

When we arrived back in Tyrone there was a lot of tension. Everyone was dying to meet Maria. They must have all suspected something was going on, but nothing was said from either side. My close friends and family knew that over the previous few months I had become a different person, and they obviously put two and two together and realized that it had to have something to do with this woman. I had somehow managed to turn my life around in a very short time, after years of neglecting myself and everyone else. I am sure I was the talk of the place, bringing home a foreign woman.

Maria, despite the language barrier, won over everyone's hearts. There would be something wrong with you if you didn't take to her, because she is a genuinely lovely, loving and caring person. She seemed to settle in with everyone very quickly.

Although she wanted to get married in her own home country, surrounded by her family and friends, she changed her mind completely when she met my mum and dad. She said that she knew they wouldn't have been able to make it over to Fagaras to see me get married, which would have been a long, tiring journey for them. So she said she would rather we got married in Omagh, with all of my family there. Also, I would have married Maria in Romania, no problem at all, but we could never have got married in a Catholic church because

Maria was divorced. That was why in the end we settled for Northern Ireland. This meant an awful lot to me because I realized what a big sacrifice she was making. Back in Romania a wedding is seen as a huge event and Maria had a lot of friends over there with whom I knew she would have loved to have spent her special day. She knew that they would have loved to see her finally settling down with someone she truly loved, who could care for her and give her a better life.

All of her friends knew me well anyway from the trips over the years. They all thought I was brilliant because I had given Andreea and Nicoletta the chance of an education and a better life outside Romania. To me, I was only doing what I felt was right because I believe that everyone should have a chance to make a better life for themselves. But in Romania, that help and support is so rare that anyone seen to be taking an interest at all is seen as a saviour.

We knew that we would hit some red tape if we were to organize a wedding in Tyrone, so we started getting things organized very quickly. There were only a very small number of people who knew we were going to settle down at all, so I decided that it was about time to tell everyone.

We didn't have a ring and as far as I was concerned not many people suspected we had a plan until one night we were in the O'Ceathain Arms with friends, and I decided there and then to get down on one knee and ask Maria publicly for her hand in marriage. I just felt an overwhelming desire to shout it from the rooftops and let everyone know that I was madly in love with this woman and I wanted to spend the rest of my life with her.

After the initial shock, Maria thought this was hilarious. She laughed and laughed and threw her arms around me and said 'Yes' once again. I felt that, although she had agreed to marry me when we spoke on the phone, it wasn't exactly the most romantic way of asking any lady for her hand in marriage. Asking her in front of my friends in a packed pub, to me showed that I was very serious about my love for her, and I wanted everyone to know how I felt.

Word spread quickly and people began coming up to me on the street, congratulating me and asking me when the big day was and how it all happened. Everyone was dying to know the latest gossip, but I didn't bat an eyelid.

My biggest concern was for my own kids and for Andreea and Nicoletta. Iulia was only a baby, so it would have meant nothing to her. She saw me all the time anyway and I would have no problem being Daddy to her. But I wanted to make sure that the older kids were OK.

Paula, Tracey and Ray already knew. It had been fairly obvious that something was going on with myself and Maria, so I had told them before I went back to Romania in March. But I left out telling Shauna because I was afraid of her reaction. I know now that was one serious mistake. One night when I had a few drinks in me I told someone, and he went and told someone else, and that someone told Shauna. I've made some mistakes in my life, but that was the biggest. Whatever kind of a hold Shauna had on me had forced me to put it off and off, and naturally enough it annoyed her that I had left her out. But I had been genuinely terrified of her reaction. After all, she was my baby.

Hearing it from a stranger sent her mad. She ranted and raved at me and let me know in no uncertain terms how unhappy she was. I couldn't explain to her at the time how difficult it was for me to break the news to her, because she wouldn't listen; she just felt humiliated. I know she felt that I was trying to replace her mother by bringing this foreign woman into our home, but it wasn't like that at all. I loved her mother and Maria knew that, but I was getting one last chance at repairing my life, rebuilding it, and I truly loved this lady.

It took a long time to rebuild the relationship between Shauna and me, and it really hurt me to see her react so badly. But she knew that I loved her and I just had to move on. The others seemed to have accepted it a bit more.

A few days after the formal announcement, Maria and I went into Omagh to look at engagement rings. She spotted the one she wanted in Paddy Laird's jewellers on Bridge Street. It was a whole five months after the original proposal over the phone, but neither of us was exactly a spring chicken, so the whole ring thing wasn't very important, as far as I was concerned. Then again, I am a man. It wasn't until we bought the ring and I saw the look of sheer happiness on Maria's face when I placed it on her finger that I realized that an engagement ring is in fact a very important thing. I think it's a woman's way of showing everyone with whom she comes in contact that the man in her life truly loves her.

As always Maria was worried about the price, insisting I wasn't to spend too much money on an engagement ring, but I would have bought any ring in the shop that day, at any cost, once it made her happy.

I knew that she couldn't wait to show it off to everyone, and somehow it made the whole wedding seem much more believable. I think that up until I bought the ring, the wedding seemed to be just a plan, an event in our heads, but I noticed how she kept looking down at her hand and admiring it all the time on the way home, saying she had never had something so beautiful and so expensive in her life.

My parents were very happy when we broke the news to them. My mother actually said it was about time I settled down again. She'd been worried about me for years, so I suppose she saw my new relationship as a bit of a lifesaver. No one said anything negative in my own immediate family, at least not to my face. To be honest, though, back then I didn't really care what anyone else thought. I had gone through years of turmoil, being in love with a woman I thought I could never have, riddled with the guilt of knowing that my children could only ever have one mother and Maria would never be Mena. But I had reached the stage where I knew that I had to start looking after, and thinking for, myself.

As parents we always put our kids first, and that's the right thing to do, but when your kids are in their twenties and have moved on with their lives, you have to start thinking about yourself. So many people stay away from getting involved in second relationships because they worry about how their adult kids will feel, but we only have one life and we have to make the most of it. I don't say this lightly, because I was torn apart with worry for years, but I say it through experience.

Maria was delighted to be getting married in Northern Ireland, despite the fact that her own family couldn't be there because of visa restrictions. In the weeks building up to the big day she was fussing around over the dress and the flowers and the usual things brides-to-be fuss over. She was very excited. I did most of the organizing, though, because Maria's English still wasn't great. There was no point in her even trying to pick up a phone to explain to someone that she was getting married and she needed x, y and z. It would have been an even bigger headache for me to have to pick up the pieces, so I just did it all myself.

We went into Enniskillen together one afternoon and she picked up a lovely green dress for the big day. She looked absolutely beautiful in it. I have to say that, after the shock of the wedding announcement died down, my own girls were great. It must have been very hard for them at the time, I know that, but they knew that, no matter what, Maria would never replace Mena. And Maria knew this herself.

Iulia wasn't too happy with all the attention Maria was getting, though. She was only five years old at the time, but she was old enough to know what she was doing, and when she was being bold. She had started to throw little tantrums all the time, screaming, crying and generally misbehaving, but the one day that sticks out in my mind was the day that we went up to the hotel to organize things. Iulia had been acting up in the car and once we got into the hotel she got worse. Then she turned around to me and stuck her teeth straight into my arm. The pain was something else.

I didn't know how to react. I wanted to shout at her but we were surrounded by people and she well knew that I was annoyed. We all knew what the problem was: she was upset that she wasn't the centre of attention and she was making her feelings known, loud and clear. Looking back now it was quite funny, but it wasn't at all funny at the time. Bit by bit, though, Iulia grew used to the idea that her mother had everyone running after her for a while and she had to take something of a back seat. But everyone loved Iulia, she was a little doll, so we all put up with the mood swings and learned to just laugh them off.

Getting married in Northern Ireland brought more problems, because I had to apply to the Home Office to get approval. Just as my luck would have it, I was turned down. It was a massive blow to us and we were devastated, but I didn't let it get the better of me. I persevered and appealed the decision. I was disgusted that we had been turned down, considering everything I had been through over the years in Northern Ireland and the lack of support we'd already had to put up with from the government when it came to arresting the bombers. I was determined to fight my corner on this and go right to the top if necessary.

Whoever received the appeal sent my information on to Pat Doherty, a Sinn Féin member of the legislative assembly, and after a lot of to-ing and fro-ing again, they eventually sent me a letter of permission, with the stipulation that we would have to get married before 4 November, when Maria's visa expired. So we set everything in motion and fixed the date for 12 October 2005.

The problem I had now was that I had to return to Romania to get permission from the Romanian government to marry in the UK. I needed a visa for Maria and Iulia. They told me that I wouldn't need to bring Andreea with me, as they could issue it without her being present. So we quickly booked flights for the three of us and we headed back out. Unfortunately, I was told when I got there that I *did* need to have Andreea with me to obtain a visa for her. She had to have her visa before 2 December, when she was due to turn 18, because if she didn't have a visa by then, she would have to return to Romania for good. Then the process of getting her out would have been an absolute nightmare.

So, I left Maria and Iulia, headed straight back to Omagh, got Andreea to pack a wee bag and we headed out again the following day to Fagaras. I was shattered when I got there. Between the journey and the stress of it all, I was absolutely drained.

Thankfully, though, it all worked out well in the end and I got all of the paperwork I needed to keep my new family with me in Omagh.

Maria and I got married in October, on the day planned, surrounded by family and friends. We held the reception at the Hunting Lodge in Baronscourt, between Newtownstewart and Drumquin.

Although it was one of the happiest days of my life, I admit that I still felt guilty – guilty that I had moved on with my life. I thought of Mena so often that day and prayed that she was giving me her blessing. It was a great day but also a difficult day in some ways for my own family, my children. It must have been hard for them to watch me stand at an altar and marry another woman. But they knew that no one would ever replace their mammy or them. I made sure they realized that from day one.

There was great excitement that morning. Nicoletta was the bridesmaid and my brother Paul was my best man. The flowers were all done by Eileen McKay, a relation of mine, and Gerard's wife, my sister-in-law Connie, made the cake. The wedding cake was totally different to what Maria would have been used to back home. All of the food was different, but she was fine with it all. The booze and the food were flowing and everyone was having a ball.

To top it all off, we had one very important guest on the day: the Sam Maguire trophy, which arrived at the wedding at 11:00 p.m. Friends of mine, Culbert Donnelly and Mickie McGoldrick from Aughnacloy, had organized everything, knowing about my love of GAA and my passion for everything about the sport. That cup being there at my wedding was simply the icing on the cake for me. It made my night.

The ceremony itself was a bit of a shock to Maria, because back in Romania the wedding kicks off at the crack of dawn on the day and lasts until about 4 o'clock the following morning, and the beer is all free, paid for by the bride and groom. In Tyrone and all over Ireland, it normally starts at 3 in the afternoon or thereabouts and ends early the next morning.

I would have gone all out and given Maria a dream day in the blink of an eye if she had wanted that, but she said she was happy to do it surrounded by my family and friends, and that was that. She loved every minute of the day and she was up dancing all night. A lot of people who had helped me over the years came to the wedding and they all said they had a great day. They seemed genuinely happy for me.

A pal of mine, John Farry, did a great job with the music on the day. He is one of my favourite local singers and he had them up on the floor all night. In fact, I was sorry to have to leave that night because the craic was mighty. I was sorry that Maria did not get to have any of her own family there on the day, but she said that she was happy once she had her girls there. I know deep down that it would have made her day to have had her family around, but some things you just cannot change.

Unfortunately, we didn't really have much of a honeymoon. The day after the wedding we headed off in the car to Knock.

Maria wanted to see what Knock was like, having heard all about it in Romania. Romania is a deeply religious country and everyone knows about Knock, Lourdes and Medjugorje. So she was very excited to be going to Knock and to be able to tell everyone back home what it was like.

She rambled in and out of the shops, picking up little statues of Holy Mary and rosary beads to send home to Fagaras, and she loved walking around the Basilica. We headed from there to Ballintragh in County Mayo. A chap I knew called John Murphy had a pub there, but when we arrived the pub was shut down. I was raging as I really wanted to meet up with John, having not seen him in years. Had he been there we would have had a reason to stay, but we decided to head from there to Bundoran in Donegal, where we stayed in a hotel there for just one night.

I went down to reception to book us in for another couple of nights, but when Maria caught me trying to pay, she went ballistic. She was so used to being cautious with her money that she said it was a waste to be spending more money on extra nights in a hotel when we had our own home to go to. It was difficult for her to get used to the idea that, although I was by no means rich, I didn't have to be counting every penny either. I wanted to stay that night because Mick Flavin and his band were playing at the hotel, and I knew that if Maria stayed on she'd have had a great night, but sure nothing would convince her to pay for even one more night. She couldn't get it into her head that we were on a holiday; all she was thinking about was saving the money.

In fact, she is still like that today. She worries all the time about money, and if she sees something in the shop for £10, she will watch that item and wait until it is reduced right down to a figure that she thinks is OK. Then she'll buy it. In fact, at the end of summer she will watch and wait for the sales and then she'll buy all the bargains she can find in a size larger for the kids so that she will have them for the following year. She is only ever happy when she feels that she's got a bargain.

When we got back home from the honeymoon, everything went back to normal immediately. My own kids were great; they really did everything they could to make Maria feel comfortable. Ray was still living with us and the girls were off doing their own things. Maria settled in fine. She had been with us for five months and in that time she had grown to love the area. She loved the house and she was busy making it her own but being careful not to go over the top. She has the height of respect for Mena and she has always made sure that there are pictures of Mena around the house.

Initially she was in shock at the size of the place, because even though it's just a normal-sized house for us it is a mansion to her, having lived in her tiny little flat for all those years. She was missing her family a little, but her days were filled with caring for the kids and shopping and she was loving every minute of it. No longer did she have to worry about where the money for the next electricity bill was coming from or how she was going to put food on the table. For once in her life, she was comfortable. In her own little world, she was rich.

It was quite odd how things changed when Maria moved into the house. In McCrea Park there hadn't been one night when something didn't happen – washing machines turning on, the kettle boiling of its own accord – and that had continued in our next two homes; but from the day Maria came to our home on Creaghmore Road, we never heard or saw another thing.

Maria said that she had the odd experience of electrical items doing their own thing, but it didn't last for long, and for me things seemed to calm down totally. Even Andreea and Nicoletta had experienced the goings-on in the first house and had told Maria about it, but it was as if there was a sort of calmness about the house after we married. The fact that everything seemed to stop made me think that maybe Mena was finally happy, knowing that I had settled down and had someone there to look after me.

Chapter 10

Happiness Tinged with Sadness

In December 2005, Tracey and her husband Mark came to the house with the best news we had heard in years: she was pregnant. My little girl was going to be a mammy and I was going to be a granddad. I was absolutely thrilled; the whole family were. It was tinged with sadness, of course, because Tracey's mammy would never get to see her grandchild, but we were all thrilled that there was going to be another little baby in the family. It was great to have something to look forward to and it lifted everyone's spirits. The girls were all talking about the pending new arrival and getting all excited about baby clothes and prams. It was a huge deal to everyone and Tracey was absolutely thrilled.

Then, out of the blue, as all the excitement was settling, just a few weeks later, Maria sat me down and told me that she thought *she* was pregnant. It was like being hit with a bolt of lightning. It was February 2006, I was becoming a granddad and, at 51 years of age, I had never thought that I would become a father again. To be brutally honest, I was shell-shocked.

Initially, Maria had done a home pregnancy test and the result was positive, but to make sure that she was definitely pregnant, she went to the doctor and, oddly enough, the sample came back negative. But despite the GP's verdict, she was still convinced that she was having a baby. She was frustrated at the surgery test and she kept telling me that she had all the symptoms of a pregnancy. Having had three other kids, she knew what it was like to 'feel' pregnant. She booked another appointment with the doctor for the following week and she was up the walls all week wondering about the outcome. When he tested her for the second time, it came back positive.

When it finally hit Maria that she was to become a mother again, she too admitted that it was the last thing she had expected. No question about it. I remember wondering if, as an older father, I would even get to see my child reach 18, as I would be hitting 70 by then. Maria was also 40 years old at this stage and we were asked if, because of her age, we wanted to have an amniocentesis test to see if everything was OK with the baby. There was a higher risk of having a baby with Down's Syndrome or some disability due to the age of the mother, and such a test would tell us if the baby had a disability. But we had a chat and decided that we didn't want to go down that road. There was also the risk of having a miscarriage with the test, and we just couldn't take that chance. We would just carry on as normal and pray that the child would be born healthy and that Maria would be OK.

It was difficult breaking the news to my children that I was to become a father again. At the end of the day they had lost their mother, their father now had another wife and now, with them all being adults, they were to have a half-brother or -sister. On top of this, Tracey would be giving birth to her baby, my grandchild, just weeks before the grandfather himself was to become a daddy again. I understand what they must have been thinking.

But when we broke the news, they were all apparently fine with it. I know in my own heart that Tracey must have been feeling bad, though, because it was her 'special time'; she was giving birth to the first grandchild in our family, the first niece or nephew for her siblings, and then all of a sudden the attention was divided between Maria and herself. I was filled with mixed emotions. I wanted this to be special for Tracey but I had to think of Maria's feelings as well. It was just another hurdle for us to get over. But we all got on with things, until we were dealt a very cruel blow.

Just a few months into her pregnancy, Tracey was delivered a bombshell. She was told that the baby's bowel was outside of her body. We knew that it was a little girl, and we had all been looking forward to her arrival, but now we had to deal with this devastating news. It was a total shock, but we were told that other children had been born with the same condition and so there was every possibility that it could be rectified. They told us that the baby would be OK while she was in the womb, but the problems would start after birth.

Fair play to Tracey and Mark, they were very strong. They tried to stay positive and we all hoped and prayed that once their little baby arrived, the surgeons could work their magic and rectify everything. But unfortunately, after she was born at full term, things just got steadily worse. We had all been staying positive, hopeful that once this little one was delivered she would be fine and Tracey herself would be OK. I didn't crowd them, Tracey and her husband. Maybe it was wrong; I'm not sure, but I didn't know what to do for the best. You'd see the wee thing lying there and some days she was breathing on her own and we all prayed that she would get better as the days went on. I remember looking into the incubators at other little babies who were also fighting for their lives and thinking how big she was compared to some of the others alongside her, and genuinely believing that she could pull through this.

But it was not to be. Her wee chest was just too narrow to expand her lungs and she lost her battle just 12 days after she was born. We were all devastated. The staff at Belfast University Hospital did everything they could possibly have done to keep her alive, but unfortunately it wasn't enough. She had no chance from day one.

The days that followed her death were terrible. Tracey had christened her little girl Mena, in memory of the grandmother she'd never know. The wee tot was cremated in the most heartbreaking ceremony I have ever encountered in my life. How they got on with their lives after that I will never know, because I know they were devastated. They had everything ready in their house to welcome their little girl back home. There were clothes, nappies, a pram, everything they needed was there for them and the hope was that they would eventually get to bring their baby home and live happily ever after as a family.

Looking back, I don't know how Tracey coped after losing little Mena. She still had to watch Maria go through her pregnancy and then little Gaby being born, and she was a beautiful healthy child, thank God. But it was heartbreaking for us all knowing that the two little girls would have grown up together all their lives and inevitably they would have been very close. I just wish things could have been different.

Maria gave birth to little Gabriella on 17 October 2006. Her arrival helped somewhat to lift all of our spirits. She is a beautiful little one, full of life, and she keeps us all on our toes. She just completed everything for us. At first we were all shocked that Maria was pregnant, but our little girl was truly a godsend. But no matter how happy we were, there was always that loss there of little Mena.

Maria now works a few hours every week and I look after the wee ones. They keep me young. I was never at home with my own children as they grew up, and I regret that to this day, but I am totally different this time around. Maybe it's my age, I'm more mellow, but all of my children know that I love them all equally. It's just that Gabriella gets completely spoiled because she is the baby, the surprise baby.

Three years after little Mena died, on the Friday before I went on holiday to Spain with the rest of the family in June 2009, I got a call from Tracey asking me to come up to the house for her little boy's birthday party, my grandson Aaron. She had given birth to Aaron a year after she lost Mena. She had a hard time during that pregnancy as well, and very nearly lost him. He finally arrived after a Caesarean section, happy and healthy. So, on the day of his second birthday, Tracey called me into a room in her home and handed me little Mena's ashes, to be placed with her grandmother in Drumquin.

I was in total shock. I just hadn't expected it, especially that day. We had mentioned it before, but it was always a hard subject to bring up, so I had decided not to mention it again, as I didn't want to upset anyone any more than they already were. But no one will ever know what it meant to me that day. I was close to tears, because I was so happy that the two of them had decided to let their little baby rest with her nanny. I went straight to the graveyard that very day and buried her with Mena, two feet under the soil, beneath the statue of the Blessed Virgin Mary. The cremation three years earlier had torn the guts out of me, to see a wee coffin disappear, my own flesh and blood, but now at least I can go out to Drumquin and say a prayer at her grave. The whole family can, and it's a very special place.

Little Mena was born on the 14th of August and died on the 26th; her granny had been murdered on the 15th. So it meant a lot to me to bury the wee one there beside her and put her name on the headstone. I know that Tracey felt so much better knowing that her mammy was looking after her little girl. It is a huge comfort to us all. They had initially planned to scatter baby Mena's ashes and I am so happy that they changed their minds. Despite all the heartbreak they endured after the birth of baby Mena, they are finally getting on with their lives, thank God, and they adore little Aaron. I often thank God that things are going well for them now.

Chapter 11

The Civil Action

When the families of those who died in Omagh started a civil action, I decided not to go down that road. A number of people whom I knew very well from the group contacted me to see what I thought, and whether I was going to come on board with them, but from the outset I was against it and I told them so. There were a few reasons why I made this choice. To my mind, the people who killed all of those innocent people in Omagh are ruthless. They have no feelings, no morals and no regard for human life. If they had wanted to bump me off for being so outspoken after the bomb, then I wouldn't have had a problem, they could have gone ahead and done it, but I worried that they could have tried to get at me through the children. My first and last thoughts were for my kids. Ray was doing his own thing and the girls were in university, and I didn't want to put any of them in danger. They had been through enough pain and misery in their short lives and I didn't want to have to put them through even more.

The decision was easy for me at the time, but I have to admit that there were brief spells over the years when I thought to myself, 'Did I make the wrong decision?' However, I was really glad that I didn't take that route when I heard that the British government had agreed to back the families who were taking the case and pay their legal fees. The reason this angered me was that it also emerged that the leader of the Real IRA, Michael McKevitt, a suspect at the time for the bombing, also had *his* legal fees paid for by the government. That turned my stomach.

The families who took the action did not by any means do it for the money, but I believe that McKevitt, Liam Campbell and the others may never serve time for the Omagh bombing and I will only be happy the day I see them behind bars. Taking them to court in a civil case, to my mind, would have amounted to nothing because it would never result in them serving a sentence.

In June 2009, McKevitt was found to be partly liable for the bomb at a High Court sitting in Belfast. Mr Justice Morgan also found Liam Campbell, Colm Murphy and Seamus Daly liable in various ways for the attack. Another suspect, Seamus McKenna, was cleared. The 12 relatives who took the case were awarded more than £1.6 million in damages for the attack. The judge also found the Real IRA liable for the bomb. He said it was clear that the bombers' primary objective was to ensure that the bomb exploded without detection, and the safety of those members of the public in Omagh town centre was of no concern to any of them. He said he was 'satisfied that those involved in the planning, preparation, planting and detonation of the bomb recognized the likelihood of serious injury or death from its detonation but decided to take that risk'.

He also said on the day that McKevitt had always held

a significant leadership role in the Real IRA and was heavily involved in the procurement of explosives at the time of the bombing. Much of this was based on evidence obtained by an undercover FBI agent, David Rupert. Mr Justice Declan Morgan also said he was satisfied that Campbell was a member of the Real IRA's Army Council in August 1998. The families who took the case were relying heavily on records and traces on two mobile phones used by the bombers on the day of the attack. The judge said the evidence proved that both Campbell and Daly were in possession of the phones before and after the attack. The case against McKenna was dismissed because it was based on hearsay evidence from his estranged wife, who was deemed an unreliable witness.

At the time, Michael Gallagher, who lost his 21-year-old son in the attack, said it was 'a result better than we could ever have imagined'. He thought it was a tremendous moral victory for the families and, while I agree with him, my wish is still to see someone go to jail, to serve a sentence for what they did.

Despite the result of this case, just as I always predicted, no one has ever been convicted in a criminal court of causing the deaths. The only man to face criminal charges over the Omagh killings was 38-year-old Sean Hoey from Jonesborough in South Armagh, and he was acquitted in 2007.

At the end of August 2009 I sent a letter to Liam Campbell in Maghaberry Prison asking him to meet up with me. He is currently being held in prison while Lithuanian authorities seek his extradition over an alleged arms smuggling plot. I told him in the letter that I wasn't seeking any vengeance, I didn't have any tricks up my sleeve and that he could have his solicitor with him if he was happy enough to meet me. I knew he'd be concerned that I could have some sort of recording device planted on me, and I told him that I too would have a solicitor with me so everything would be above board.

I informed him that I had three questions for him. I wanted to know if he was involved in the bombing and, if he was, what did he think it achieved. I also asked if he knew of any government agencies that may have colluded with the bombers and if he felt that he was used as a political football to help Sinn Féin get where they were today. I felt if he had nothing to hide, then he had nothing to fear in meeting me. But unfortunately he never replied, just like so many other people whom I have contacted about this over the years.

Civil cases have a much lower burden of proof, with the judge reaching his or her verdict on the balance of probabilities. The difference in criminal law is that guilt must be proved beyond reasonable doubt, and I genuinely don't believe we will ever see that happen.

I feel connected to three groups in Ireland now: the families in Omagh, the families of those killed in the Monaghan and Dublin bombings, and the families of those killed on Bloody Sunday. I truly believe that the Irish government know exactly who carried out the Monaghan/Dublin bombings; the British government know who murdered those innocents killed on Bloody Sunday; and the Irish government, the Gardaí, the Police Service of Northern Ireland (PSNI) and the British Secret Service know exactly who murdered those people on 15 August 1998, but they are not prepared to do anything about it. The people from these groups, in my mind, will never see justice. As far as I can see, the peace process is more important than human life.

They talk about a united Ireland, and it's only a matter of time before the Catholics out-vote the Protestants because they have more children, but there will never be a united Ireland, despite all the talk of it, because the rest of Ireland doesn't want us. They have enough problems of their own, enough hooligans running around the streets without having our lot down as well. I believe that if there was a vote in the Republic tomorrow on whether to have a united Ireland, it would be an emphatic 'No.' And it would be an emphatic 'no' in the North as well, even on the Nationalist side.

It really gets to me when I hear politicians – Nationalists, Republicans, Unionists and Loyalists – saying at the end of the day that we're all human beings. I hate being classed as a Nationalist. I'm a Catholic, and so what? I remember being in a pub one day in London and the man beside me, who knew who I was, leaned over to me and whispered into my ear, 'I'm a Catholic.' I turned to him and said, 'I don't care what you are. It makes no difference one way or another to me.' If we keep going on like this we will never move on. It is so pathetic.

Back in 1998, Omagh was falling to pieces. Now it's a thriving town. It's heartbreaking to think that such a massive tragedy created such a huge boom. And it's horrible to think the people who died will never get to see the massive transformation, because the truth of the matter is that it might never have happened had they not been killed. Omagh District Council built a fancy memorial garden with murals in it and a big pool in the middle of it, and it hasn't worked since the day it went up. They spent something like £400,000 on it and it's simply a urinal for lads coming out of the pubs late at night. My family, and most of the other families I have spoken to, didn't want that sort of memorial. Hillsborough was the same, as was Dunblane, and I don't think the families left behind in those towns either had much say in what went on with the fund.

In fact, I asked that a very special plaque be placed in this garden and no one had the decency to get back to me. It now sits on a wall in the office of the Omagh Support and Self-help Group, and we are proud to have it there. This plaque, which has a prayer on it in memory of those killed, was handed over to me in 2008, just before the ten-year anniversary of the Omagh bombing, by a police officer from New York, Stephen McDonald, who was shot in the neck in 1986 and left paralysed from the neck down. He had also lost one of his best friends, a priest, Father Mychal F Judge, in the September 11th 2001 attacks.

Stephen McDonald came to Omagh shortly after the bombing and returned with the plaque in 2008. He made such a huge impact on my life, so much of an impact that when I arrived back home on the day, I cried and cried. Maria thought something had happened to me because I was inconsolable. This man had met with the person who had destroyed his life all those years ago, and yet he held no grudge. He forgave that man for ruining his life, and that to me was a huge feat.

People may ask why I can't be like that man, why I can't just forgive and forget, but I can't. I wish I could, because it would make things much easier for me, but people are different and I am who I am. But I admired that man so much for his heart. He shook my hand on the day he handed over that plaque and his words were so comforting. Despite all that he had lost, he still had time to come to us and offer his support. That to me is a God-given gift and I truly believe that man is an angel on this Earth.

But we, the victims of the bombing, never wanted anything but justice for what happened to us. Yet some families were offered ridiculous sums, as if it were meant to make it all better. Godfrey Wilson lost his daughter and he got a miserly £7,500. My own son Ray got nothing, not a shilling, because he wasn't in Omagh on the day, even though he lost his mother. Those who were injured got some money – and don't get me wrong, I am not saying for one minute that they don't deserve to get money for what they went through – but my argument is that once a person is dead, they are dead and yet there was no financial sum there for the families who would never see their loved ones again.

I remember reading about a woman killed in a car crash in England whose family got £1 million. We didn't get anything like that. If Mena had been a solicitor or held a high-profile job, we would have got a huge sum of money, but because she was a housewife we got nothing.

The families who got small amounts of money from the government will at least get something from the civil case, if money ever becomes available. However, it was rumoured that if you received, say, £100,000 initially from the government and then £200,000 from the civil case, the government could technically request the first sum back. Unfortunately, no one knows how it will work until it actually happens. But those who got awarded sums from the civil case believe they will never see any money, despite winning the case, because the people who have been ordered to pay out won't have the money to do it. But maybe we will all be proved wrong someday. At the end of the day, what those families wanted was some form of justice, some way of pointing at these people and having the courts recognize their part in the bombing, and that has happened. And that made it all worthwhile. Money isn't everything.

But people had to go through a lot to get to that stage. I remember one woman who was badly injured in the bombing standing up in court and being asked by a solicitor to take off her top so that they could see the scars on her back from the blast. It was an absolute disgrace what people were put through. She was offered a small amount of money, which she turned down, but fair play to that woman, she went on to another court and she got £200,000. They treated some of the survivors like dirt. They showed no respect whatsoever for anyone.

For my own part, I will not let things rest. I have sent letters over the years to all the politicians and I am still getting nowhere. I thought the leader of Fine Gael in the Republic, Enda Kenny, was a genuine man, but my thoughts were put into question when, after writing him a letter, he didn't even have the decency to write back. I sent the same letter to the Irish Taoiseach, Brian Cowen, and although I have had no positive response from him, his office did send a letter back saying they had received the letter and I would be responded to in due course, whatever that means, a standard reply no doubt. I also sent Gordon Brown a letter outlining my frustration at how things had gone in relation to the inquiry, and I sent David Cameron a copy of that letter. I got no reply from either of these men.

It just goes to show that once you are dead and gone, no matter how you die, you are dead and gone forever. Neither I nor anyone else who has lost a loved one in a terrorist attack will ever change that. Until they lose a loved one in similar circumstances, politicians will never understand how important it is to acknowledge people and let them know that you do actually have a heart, even if the truth of the matter is that you couldn't care less. The more time goes by, the less everyone will care.

Chapter 12

How Life Changes

Despite all the events in my life, I have continued with my charity work both abroad and at home. It all keeps me going. I was the president of the local St Vincent de Paul for more than seven years, but there came a time when I decided to step down; as they say, it's always good to bring in some new blood. I am now vice-president of the branch in Drumquin and it gives me a bit more time to myself to do other things. One of our local priests, Father Devine, got me into the St Vincent de Paul Association a year after Mena died. I think he did it to help get my mind off things. That's the sort of person he is. I started off like everyone else, just as a member, and then somehow I was voted onto the committee and have been there ever since. SVDP is very strong in Northern Ireland. It's busier than ever now, as the recession has affected most people and many are finding themselves unemployed and struggling to survive. For couples with young children it's all the harder with the cost of school uniforms, books, lunches, etc., on top of everything else. We call out to these families to see what their circumstances are, and it is up to us to make sure that whomever we choose to help out deserves that help.

I would love to see more people, especially young people, getting involved in the Association, because it gives you a great sense of satisfaction. It's also a great way of getting to know people. I know that I would more than likely never have done anything like this had Mena been alive. It would have been the sort of thing that she would have done gladly, but I don't think it would have been me. I am delighted that I took up Father Devine's offer, because I have got to meet many very nice and genuinely caring people over the years through the Association and I love the work.

When it comes to my sporting life, though, I'm afraid my days of refereeing are well and truly over. I just lost the will to carry on after I lost Mena. It all culminated when I came out of hospital after having an operation on my stomach. I had been very sick in the weeks and months prior to the op and I felt very out of sorts when I got out. I tried to push myself to get back out there and start afresh, but my heart just wasn't in it.

I could see that people's attitudes to me on and off the pitch had changed since the bombing. People were trying to be nice, and I appreciate that, but I knew that it would never be the same for me again after losing Mena. I went to referee a GAA match shortly after I got out of hospital and as I arrived on the pitch the two teams applauded me. I knew they were genuinely being caring, and I appreciated it at the time, but I just didn't feel right. I played out the game and I knew there was a totally different reaction to me than normal.

I went on the following Saturday morning to referee a soccer match and the same thing happened. That went on and on until one day in Ardboe when I was refereeing the Ardboe and Mooretown Derby. Normally at these games it would be hell for leather, with teams nearly ending up in fist fights, but that morning I heard one of the managers saying, 'It's Kevin today, boys, so don't be out there annoying him. He has enough trouble.' When the game was over, I picked up my kit bag, threw it into the boot of the car and said to myself, 'That's it.' I'd had enough.

I was no longer the bastard dressed in black; I was the referee who lost his wife. 'Leave him alone' was the message, and it killed the game for me. I was happier when they were calling me filthy names through the wire or shouting them over to me before I even got out of the car. I loved that. I loved being told to 'feck off' because someone wasn't happy with the way I had made a judgement. It was all part of the game. And suddenly it was gone and I knew that I could never get that back.

Once it stopped, it just took the whole interest out of it. When I took my refereeing courses, in soccer particularly, I was told that the day you walk off the field and you haven't enjoyed the game, that's the day you should hang up your boots and pack it all in. I only ever did refereeing because I loved it. I loved the banter on the pitch with the lads, the arguments before the game and the arguments after it. For me it was an adrenalin rush. Even when they were screaming abuse at me for not noticing what they all had seen – a player running offside or a ball going over the line – I carried on, loving every minute of it. The abuse never got to me because I knew that it was par for the course to be hated as a referee. No one loves the fella in black. Both sides think that you're on the other team's side. You can't win. But that was the whole fun of it. And I just didn't get that kick any more. It took the whole edge off it.

Even though I walked of my own accord, I do miss it. I miss the banter with the lads and the few drinks in the pub after the game. But as they say, all good things must come to an end, and I knew that my time was up.

I still raise funds for people in Romania. Even though I haven't been back myself since Maria came to live with me, I get the lads from the support group to take food, clothes and toys over for me. It keeps me going. There are about five families over there whom I still help and they rely on that help, so it's not something I will be stopping soon. I'm not half as involved as I used to be, but I still do my bit. Just before Christmas 2009 we organized a big load to go off to Romania and we managed to get a lorry free of charge to take everything over for us. We had spent weeks organizing this truck-load of relief, but when we heard that it had arrived safely and everyone was delighted, it made it all worthwhile. It gives me a great sense of relief to know that I am still doing my bit for people in Romania, who have so much less than us. I will continue doing this for as long as I can move.

When Maria flies out, she often takes some clothes and things herself and she meets with people over there and finds out what they need, so I don't see my work ending there in the near future. There is always something to do, someone who needs a bit of a helping hand.

It's one thing I have to say about Northern Ireland, the people are the salt of the earth. When someone within the community is faced with tragedy, everyone gets together to give whatever they can afford, be it a hundred pounds or one pound, and we are grateful for whatever they have. I think their generosity is because we have all been through hell and back over the years, even those not directly affected by the bombings, and had to live with the after-effects, and it definitely changed us as a community. I don't think there is another area in this country where people are more caring and more giving, and I am very proud to live here.

The End

I made my last trip back to Romania in August of 2007. I intend going back again over the next couple of years, but I went back that time for Nicoletta's wedding. It was probably the worst holiday of my life, simply because I couldn't cope with the heat. It was just stifling. I couldn't walk anywhere without pumping sweat down my face, down my back, down my legs. It was a nightmare. I swore never, ever to visit the country in the height of summer again, because as an Irishman I'm just not used to that sort of mad heat.

Nicoletta is two years older than Andreea, and she was the first of the girls to marry, so I knew that the wedding would be a big deal for her family back in Fagaras but I never actually realized just *how* big a deal that would be. I'd had the experience of being at Ovideo's marriage to Maria and thought that was an eye-opener, but this one just took the biscuit for being totally over the top. The celebrations started at about 10 o'clock that morning as the crowds started arriving at the flat. It was absolute mayhem. The actual ceremony wasn't to start until

5 o'clock that afternoon, but there was no such thing as the guests spending the day getting spruced up. No, this lot must have thrown on the make-up and got dressed the night before, because they were knocking at the door at the crack of dawn, singing and dancing.

Within a couple of hours the place was packed to the rafters. I had to get out because it was getting hotter and hotter by the minute as the crowds kept swelling into the little flat. There wasn't an inch of space left to move around. I was forced to stand out on the street, with the blazing sun literally blistering my skin. As I stood there with the sweat running down my back, I looked around and noticed that none of them was bothered at all by this heatwave. The poor pale Irishman, on the other hand, was dying of heat exhaustion.

Then all of a sudden this band arrived on the scene and they started blaring music out, dreadful music that would turn you deaf if you stayed around long enough. Between the noise of the guests yabbering on and the screech of this so-called band, I thought I was going to go mad. Looking back on it now I laugh, because I must have just looked like this grumpy old man from Ireland who was pumping sweat all the time and looking as if he was fit to kill.

The music went on all day and all night! Nico paid something like €2,000 for this group and that amount of money in Romania could keep some families going for a year. Yet I'd have paid them that, and more, to pack up and leave. I think I was just too old and too ignorant to sit back and make the most of it, and they all slag me off about it now. If it had been a bit cooler I think I would have managed, but my age and my white skin didn't help the situation at all.

Early in the afternoon the bride was taken off to meet the groom-to-be to sign the register in the local office. Everyone followed her through the town to the registry office and they were all singing and dancing. I couldn't wait to get off to the church for a bit of shade and peace and quiet, but there was no hurry with this lot. As they all posed for photos outside, smiling away with the sun baking down on us, I was left there to melt!

Eventually, we all headed off to the church. This is where the real nightmare began for me. We got to the chapel and more photos were taken in the sweltering sun while we all had to stand there smiling away, looking all cool when in fact I was about to collapse. Eventually we made our way inside the church, where I was praying for a bit of air-conditioning. But of course it never came. Everyone else was standing around, for an hour and a half, smiling and looking all relaxed, and I was about to faint. In fact, I got so bad that I had to go to the back of the church and drink the holy water out of the font.

I hadn't thought of bringing any water in with me, as I was under the illusion that the ceremony would last an hour at the most, but I honestly thought that I would end up in hospital that day from dehydration and heat exhaustion. When the Mass was over there was more dancing and singing on the streets and more photos posed for in the blistering heat before we finally headed off for the reception.

If I thought Maria's wedding had been a bit mad, I hadn't bargained for what was to follow. If you were a lover of Romanian music you were in your element, but for an auld fella like myself, you couldn't hear yourself think, never mind talk. The food was going all night; maybe five different meals were served. There was no such a thing as eating and then dancing; over there, you ate and danced at the same time.

There was vodka, whiskey, gin, beer and any drink you could name, and you literally drank as much as you wanted at the expense of the bride and the groom. And everyone there drank and ate until they dropped. But this old man just wanted to go home to bed.

They were all talking about the wedding cake, which was absolutely huge: layers upon layers of sponge and icing. It was unbelievable; about nine tiers in total. I remember Maria being shocked at our wedding cake when she saw it back in Tyrone, because it was an ordinary fruit and icing cake, three tiers, and nothing like the Romanian delicacy. It was the typical Irish wedding cake, but Maria was so used to having big, over-the-top cakes, that she stood staring at it, wondering if it really was the actual wedding cake.

When the dancing started that night, the groom's parents got up on the floor and started the ritual of throwing money at the happy couple. There was wad upon wad of cash being thrown at the newlyweds, and it wasn't Romanian leu; no, this was literally hundreds upon hundreds, maybe even a thousand euro at a time. Then it was the turn of the aunts and uncles to make their donation and, just like the parents, they threw wads of either euro or sterling; some even had dollars. Even though times are hard in Romania, somehow the families always seem to manage to come up with some money on a wedding day. Some of these families actually go into debt at this time, but it is seen as an important tradition to start a newlywed couple off on their new path. No amount of money is too big or too small.

The way it works over there is that if the groom's father throws in €1,000, then the father of the bride – me in this case – would have to match it; and if the groom's mother throws in another €1,000, then Maria has to match that. I didn't take part in this ceremony because I had given them their money before they got married, so I had a lucky escape. But the same rule applies to the cousins on each side as well, and basically any guest who wants to donate to the cause. There were no irons or electric kettles accepted in Fagaras. Not a chance. So it must have been hilarious for Maria to see what gifts we give in Ireland for a wedding present; there's no thousands here to be thrown into a pot. But in fairness, this is the custom in that country and it's the only time that you will see 'big money' being dished out in Romania. No matter how poor the families are, they will do everything in their power to give their children the send-off they believe they deserve, and may save up for years and years for that day.

The rest of them had a ball as the night went on but I couldn't wait to get out and back home. Between the heat on the day and all the excitement, I was shattered. At around 11:00 p.m. they held a massive fireworks display, which must have cost another small fortune, and that went on until the wee hours of the morning, just like the drinking. Most of them stayed on until they could stand no more.

Luckily for me, Gaby fell asleep and so I made my escape. But believe it or not, the drinking and the dancing started all over again the next morning, all the drink for free. I don't know how people do it over there, but when they do, they do it big.

Despite all my moaning it was a great day for Nico and her family and it was great to see them all enjoying themselves, forgetting about all their worries and just living life.

Maria, myself, Andreea, Iulia and Gaby had gone over for the wedding. The other kids stayed at home. But despite the weather and the mania, it was a nice break.

Maria goes back and forth now, visiting her own family, but she has two sisters living in Northern Ireland now and that's a great help. One sister in particular she sees quite a lot. It's amazing how they all settled in so well, got jobs and are rearing their families. They may have been surrounded by aunts and uncles and lifelong friends in Fagaras, but unfortunately the prospects of a good and comfortable future would have been very low, so it is great to see them in their lovely homes now and settling in within the community.

On many an occasion I have sat and thought about how things have changed for me, and I have come to the conclusion that everything in life happens for a reason. In my heart of hearts I truly believe that it was Mena who set all of this in motion. I had no knowledge of or interest in Romania when she suggested we take a child for a summer holiday. If it wasn't for her insisting that we should get involved in the Romanian project and setting the ball rolling herself, then none of this would have happened.

It goes without saying that if I could have turned the clock back and brought Mena back into our lives, I would have done it in the blink of an eye, but unfortunately life isn't that easy. But I do believe that Mena sent Maria to me; beyond a shadow of a doubt. In my mind, it was all simply a matter of fate.

It has taken me many years and I have gone down many a bad road, but thank God I am now finally moving on with my life. It's been very hard to turn things around and I have faced all sorts of demons over the years, but thankfully I got through it fairly intact. My saving grace was handing over that shotgun when I did, because if I had gone ahead and pulled that trigger, I would have simply caused nothing but misery and suffering for my children.

I would never have seen my lovely daughter marry and my beautiful grandson grow up into the lively little fella he is today. I would never have had the chance to make the most of what I have left, never got the chance to travel to Romania, see what life was like for people who, through no choice of their own, were born with nothing and lived with nothing. And, most importantly, I would never have met Maria and become a father again, not just to Maria's own three children but to another little beauty, Gabriella.

I believe that child came into my life to make a difference. I truly believe that she was a gift from above. Having Gaby no doubt made our marriage stronger, and I believe she also arrived to help smooth over the cracks within my own family. You could not help but love her, and all of our other children absolutely adore her.

Suicide may seem like an easy way out when things get so difficult that you can't for love nor money see another option. But because I have been down that road myself, on more than one occasion, I can say that it's by no means an easy way out, if you take the time to stop and think about what you will leave behind.

Hard as it may seem at the time, you have to try to consider how your loved ones would feel if you went ahead and ended it all. If I had killed myself, I would have destroyed my own children's lives and I would never have had the chance to help so many young deprived children in Romania. I understand how some people get to that stage, but I would urge anyone feeling like this to seek help. You cannot always go it alone in life.

When I was in the depths of despair, I had no idea that just a short journey down the road would lead me to love and a whole new life. My mind was consumed by what was happening at that very moment, how depressed I was and how I felt the world had dealt me the worst blow ever. I never once thought that I could change not only my own life, but the lives of many other people, many miles away. I was so boxed in at the time that I could see nothing but the end of the road and I wanted to end my journey. I wasn't even thinking, 'What if I just get through this year?' That never occurred to me once. I just wanted out and that was that. But somehow, and I don't know how, I managed to open my mind to the possibility that things might just improve in my life and I made a concerted effort to make that happen. To let someone else help, let them in.

I had gone to Tom, the counsellor in the Tara Centre, on and off over the years, simply to pacify Shauna, but I hadn't really opened up to him. To be quite honest, I thought he was crap on those first few visits. I remember thinking to myself many a time, 'Sure, what the hell would *he* know about how I am feeling and what I'm going through?' The truth was, I just wasn't ready for it. It wasn't my time and my mind wasn't open to moving on. But, thanks to Shauna, I persevered. And in time, I recognized my need for that man's help and I started to open up.

I ended up spending an hour at a time with this counsellor who, only weeks earlier, I believed to be a waste of time. At first I spent my sessions just talking about the kids and losing Mena and how I felt that I would never see justice for her. Then one day I went into his office and I saw four big cushions on the floor shaped out like a square. I remember thinking, 'What is this fella playing at?' He started talking to me and he pointed to the cushions and he told me to look down at the cushions on the floor. He told me that I was actually slap-bang in the centre of those cushions, hemmed in, blocked in on all sides, and I knew there and then that he was right.

He made me sit up and think that day about what I was actually doing to myself. That was the day when I just blurted it all out. I told him in detail how I felt. I had told him on a previous visit how I had fallen for this woman head over heels and how I had been fighting with my feelings for years, but I hadn't told him everything. I just said it as a passing comment the odd time. But as I looked down at those four cushions, acting as barriers, it dawned on me there and then that he was 100 per cent right.

I realized that if I didn't do something about this mess I was in, I would never get better. I would never get out of that box. He told me that day to stop thinking about what everyone else thought of me. He told me that it was my life and I had to do what was right for me and not what others felt was right for me. He changed my life that day. He was a huge help to me. It was on that day that I decided to stop acting as if I was the child in the family and start behaving like an adult. I knew that I had to make a stand and that no one could run my life but me.

At this time I spoke to David, Paula's husband, and I confided in him about my feelings for Maria. Fair play to that chap, for he told me that day to do what I wanted with my life. He said the kids had all moved on and it was time for me, no matter what anyone else thought, to try to move on as well. Between Tom and David, I knew that I had to make a decision and I had to make that decision based on my own thoughts and nobody else's.

I now know for a fact that my life was mapped out for me, from the day I met Mena until the day she died and right up until now. I cannot change fate; no one can. What happened in my life was meant to happen in my life, however hard and disastrous it may have felt at the time.

Although I am very bitter and will remain bitter to the day I die, I am also very grateful for the life I had with Mena. She was the love of my life; there is no doubt about it. That is by no way taking anything away from Maria; I love her for many different reasons. But Mena was my first love, she gave me four beautiful children who I am so proud of and I will always love her 'til the day I die.

People say we should move on, forgive and forget, but I will never forgive the people who killed her and who scarred mine and Mena's youngest child, and I have no qualms about admitting that. They destroyed all of our lives. But I cannot judge them. The man above will do that in his own time. To be honest, I don't know how they sleep in their beds at night knowing the damage they have done and the heartbreak they have caused. But I have to accept that they must have no conscience. My wish is that one day someone out there who knows what happened that day, knows who was responsible, will go to the police and will give them the evidence needed to convict. Unfortunately, though, I have to accept that that day may never come.

One thing I know for sure is that we are all only on loan in this world and I am very grateful for the life I had with Mena.

She was most definitely my better half. My whole world was turned upside-down the day of the bombing and, although it tore me apart, it also made me realize how precious life is and how important family and friends are as you continue your journey.

It's horrible to think that it takes something horrendous like a bomb to make you sit up and think, but that is what happened to me. My children will all agree that I am a better father now than I ever was when Mena was alive. I left all the parenting to her. I paid the bills and put food on the table. I was the main provider, but she kept everything else ticking over. She was a fantastic mother. But it took me a long time to realize that paying the bills is not the only role of a father, and I know she kept that whole household and our family running every single day of our married life, singlehanded.

I know that my children suffered hugely over the years, and I know at times I was of no help to them whatsoever, but they know that I have always and always will love them. They are my reason for living.

It can be hard for a man to open up at times to his feelings, and I wouldn't be the best in the world at saying how I feel, but I want my children to know that even if I don't say it enough, I love them with all my heart. I have brought other children, someone else's children, into their lives and I love those girls to bits as well, but I never want my own flesh and blood to think that I have replaced them. Those kids are what kept me going when I was at my worst ebb, and they are what I live for every single day.

I am eternally grateful for meeting Maria. She saved me at a time when I felt I had absolutely nothing to live for. Mena sent me to Fagaras; I have no doubt whatsoever about that. I truly believe that she is my guardian angel and she wanted me to be happy after she left. In my mind, she sent Maria to me. Although I fought my feelings for all those years, I can honestly say that I am truly happy, happier than I have been in many, many years. I have my extended family all around me and they are all healthy and happy.

My lifestyle has also improved tenfold. My drinking is well under control. I still have the odd few pints but nothing like what I would have drunk over those horrible years. I now have something to live for and I know I drank myself into a stupor because I felt my life was over.

There is nothing I love more now than being at home with the kids. They all keep me going. Nicoletta now has her own little baby as well; she went through a rough time with the birth, just like our Tracey, but thank God it all went well in the end and she had a healthy little girl called Nicole.

I go up to Mena's grave every Friday at 6 o'clock. It's a special time for me and I love to go up on my own and have time to think. The only occasions I miss visiting is when I am away on holiday. I leave the house every Friday evening to head up to the Credit Union in Drumquin and then I make my way to the cemetery. Every single time I go to walk out the door, Maria will shout after me, 'Have you got the cangla?' It's her way of saying 'candle'. I put a candle on Mena's grave every week, which burns for seven days. If I'm away, my mother goes up on the Friday evening to replace it. I will continue to do that every week for as long as there is a breath in my body.

Maria knows that Mena was the love of my life and she doesn't have a problem with that at all. In fact, Maria always asks me how the grave is when I get back; she is a very caring person. I'm sure that if Mena were alive today and she met Maria, just in passing, the two of them would get on great. Both of them are caring, considerate people.

If I had one wish now it would be that my family could grow up in a Northern Ireland with no bigotry or hatred. There was a time when I would have to worry about that solely from the point of view of Catholics and Protestants, but I have even more to worry about now, because there are people, and some of these are extreme xenophobes, standing up and speaking out against foreign people and it does have an effect on how people treat others, how they treat people from Romania, Poland, Latvia.

I worry about how the girls feel when they hear these comments. The worrying thing is that some people listen to this sort of bigoted preaching and they accept what these people say as gospel. That is difficult for me. You also see others speaking out about gays and lesbians, belittling them, and I think it's a disgrace because we are all human beings and we all deserve respect.

I would love people of all religions, all races, all sexes, to be able to walk down the street without having to worry about being beaten up or abused. I would love to forget about all this politics of 'green' and 'orange'. To this day, people are still refused jobs in the North because of their surnames, and that has to change. Just because you don't hear about bombs exploding in Northern Ireland every other day does not mean that it's a peaceful place. Far from it. We still have our problems and it doesn't look as though they will be going away anytime soon.

At the moment, things are quiet enough in the North when it comes to acts of terrorism. We are all somehow living together and rebuilding our lives after all the years of death and destruction. But I am very worried that at some stage in the not-so-distant future, this will all change. I feel there is something simmering and it's only a matter of time before it all kicks off.

There are still areas of tension around the North and it only takes a few ignorant people to start the violence and intimidation up again. I don't care what happens to me in this life, but I will fight for my family until the day I die.

I lost my first wife through violence and a lack of respect for the value of life, and I am not prepared to lose anyone else in this country. When it comes to justice in Northern Ireland, in my mind there is none. The governments both north and south of the border are to blame for that. If the Prime Minister of either country lost a loved one in a bombing, you can be sure that in a matter of weeks, not years, someone would be behind bars for the crime. But we are the little people, and in my mind that makes a huge difference in the eyes of the law. If those killed that day had been dignitaries, flying in from abroad on government business, those responsible would be locked away in a prison cell indefinitely to rot. But that's life.

I cannot change things myself, but I pray that people of all races, of all cultures, can eventually live together in peace with no interference from anyone else. 'Live and let live' is my motto. It won't happen overnight, but I pray that one day it does.

Today I am very grateful for what I have. Over the years I have loved and lost, and losing Mena was the one thing that very nearly tipped me over the edge. But thank God my life has moved on. I am happier now than I have been in years. I know that Mena is my angel, and I truly believe that she sent Maria into my life to get me back on track. I now sleep peacefully each night knowing that I am safe, in the comfort of her wings.

Hay House Titles of Related Interest

Everyday Angels,
by Jenny Smedley

I Can See Angels,
by Jacky Newcomb

Left to Tell,
by Immaculée Ilibagiza

Mozart's Ghost,
by Julia Cameron

Saving Samantha,
by Samantha Weaver

Why Do Bad Things Happen?,
by Gordon Smith

Why Kindness Is Good for You,
by David Hamilton

We hope you enjoyed this Hay House book.
If you would like to receive a free catalogue featuring additional
Hay House books and products, or if you would like information
about the Hay Foundation, please contact:

Hay House UK Ltd
292B Kensal Road • London W10 5BE
Tel: (44) 20 8962 1230; Fax: (44) 20 8962 1239
www.hayhouse.co.uk

***

Published and distributed in the United States of America by:
Hay House, Inc. • PO Box 5100 • Carlsbad, CA 92018-5100
Tel: (1) 760 431 7695 or (1) 800 654 5126;
Fax: (1) 760 431 6948 or (1) 800 650 5115
www.hayhouse.com

***

Published and distributed in Australia by:
Hay House Australia Ltd • 18/36 Ralph Street • Alexandria, NSW 2015
Tel: (61) 2 9669 4299, Fax: (61) 2 9669 4144
www.hayhouse.com.au

***

Published and distributed in the Republic of South Africa by:
Hay House SA (Pty) Ltd • PO Box 990 • Witkoppen 2068
Tel/Fax: (27) 11 467 8904
www.hayhouse.co.za

***

Published and distributed in India by:
Hay House Publishers India • Muskaan Complex • Plot No.3
B-2 • Vasant Kunj • New Delhi - 110 070
Tel: (91) 11 41761620; Fax: (91) 11 41761630
www.hayhouse.co.in

***

Distributed in Canada by:
Raincoast • 9050 Shaughnessy St • Vancouver, BC V6P 6E5
Tel: (1) 604 323 7100
Fax: (1) 604 323 2600

***

Sign up via the Hay House UK website to receive the Hay House
online newsletter and stay informed about what's going on with your
favourite authors. You'll receive bimonthly announcements
about discounts and offers, special events, product highlights,
free excerpts, giveaways, and more!
www.hayhouse.co.uk